This is an important book. It hits all the crucial points about grooming and the inner thoughts of the victim.
Sue Atkinson, author of _Climbing out of Depression_

This book is beautifully written but shocking and tragic in content. It is difficult to read and it is very difficult not to break down when reading it. This story... will remain with me for a very long time.
Baroness Elizabeth Butler-Sloss GBE

This book is unique. Written through the eyes of a child, it brings out so clearly the gamut of emotions – delight, confusion, fear – that the child experienced, as well as how she attempted to disassociate herself from all of it. It shows just how devious the "Uncle Georges" are: how their grooming behaviour draws in the child who longs to feel special and loved, to feel grown up.

I strongly recommend this emotionally charged and challenging book to anyone who has experienced child abuse and to the many people in all walks of life who are trying to understand the devastating, long-term suffering caused by it. Child counsellors and psychotherapists will find it especially useful.
Pauline Pearson, Churches' Child Protection Advisory Service

This extraordinary book captures the deep emotions without bombarding the reader with sordid details. It has helped me to understand how children and their families can be groomed so effectively by skilled and determined paedophiles; and why and how those who have been hurt in this way can cover the events so deeply and for so long.
Andrew Billington, Director of the Jack Petchey Foundation

I was in a different family in a different country, in a different room with different wallpaper, but I recognize the maze of distortions, collusions and concealments that build into a high security prison. When someone begins to visit her prison with the gift of permission, then healing begins. I was able to get past my own reticence about reading about trauma because *Goodbye Pink Room* is written with the clarity and incomprehension of a child of God; she held my hand but did not push me. This book gives courage and fuel to all survivors by its powerful message, that it is grace that opens the bolts of a prison."
An adult survivor, still a victim

Powerful, sensitive, moving, honest account of a girl's experience of sexual abuse, this book presents a forthright challenge for anyone working with young people, presenting an alarming reality that cannot be ignored.
Childrenswork **magazine**

I was hooked from page one and devoured it avidly. I was constantly awed by the restraint with which the author hinted at the depths of Rose's suffering and the blindness of those who should have been protecting and encouraging her. Having been taken inside Rose's head and heart as she learns to dissociate in order to survive, I was grateful for the final chapters with their movement towards a way of living with the totally "un-liveable-with".

This is truly an extra-ordinary book – hyphen deliberate. I shall be recommending it to colleagues and clients for many years to come.
Alison Balaam, Counsellor MA (Cantab), Dip Humanistic Counselling, BACP Accredited Counsellor (2004)

This book highlights how parents can actually make a child more vulnerable to grooming and abuse. Parents fail to see the real threat nearer to home. Anyone currently involved with children, or helping adult survivors of abuse, would benefit from reading it.
Eileen Hurst, Social Worker

So well written… a powerful message that I believe the church needs to hear. People who have read *Pathway Through Pain* know Jane's gift of describing truly and honestly how things really are.
Angela Newton, Counsellor

This book *IS* extraordinary. Very powerfully written. No wonder it took fourteen years.
Alison Kidd, MA, PhD

This book is a real gift to those of us who were oblivious to what we can now learn through it.

I had no idea of the immensity of the horror of abuse until I read this book. I found it intensely moving. It conveyed so much of the agony of it. And there is so much abuse about: people need to know the horror. Although I could hardly bring myself to continue reading it, I could not put it down either. Jane has an extraordinary gift for describing in words the indescribable.

…That little girl with her sincere, eager faith. No wonder adult survivors say that life after abuse is peppered with such internal pain. This book explains why and I've never read such a clear explanation. Rose was paying the cost not twice over, but a lifetime over.

This book has brought an inkling of understanding to me in my safe life. Thank you. Thank you.
Eliza Treasure, an "ordinary" lady in her eighties

As a GP I see many people like "Rose": they come to me because they need help. This book is a most remarkable story and achievement. It enables me to understand what's going on inside them; how experiences might have felt for the child, and how they still feel for the grown-up. And the big questions: Where was God when it happened? Where is He now? Jane addresses them without any flimflam. It ends so very honestly and powerfully. It's a truly amazing book.

Dr Jenny Durandt, General Practitioner

This is one of the most important books published in the last thirty years.

The writer has disappeared, leaving the child to speak so clearly and naturally with precision and power and the beauty of devastating simplicity.

Right Reverend Donald Allister, Bishop of Peterborough

This is essential reading for all those who don't "get it".

Elizabeth Hall, National Safeguarding Officer for the Church of England & Methodist Church

goodbye pink room

as told to
Jane Grayshon

Foreword by Elizabeth Hall

L I O N

Published by Lion Books
an imprint of
Lion Hudson plc
Wilkinson House, Jordan Hill Road,
Oxford OX2 8DR, England
www.lionhudson.com/fiction

ISBN 978 0 7459 5646 6
e-ISBN 978 0 7459 5799 9

First edition 2012

Acknowledgments
pp. 93, 123 Scripture quotations are taken from the Holy Bible, New
Living Translation, copyright © 1996, 2004, 2007 by Tyndale House
Foundation. Used by permission of Tyndale House Publishers, Inc.,
Carol Stream, Illinois 60188. All rights reserved.

p. 203 Scripture quotation taken from the Holy Bible, New
International Version, copyright © 1973, 1978, 1984 International
Bible Society. Used by permission of Hodder & Stoughton, a member
of the Hodder Headline Group. All rights reserved. "NIV" is a
trademark of International Bible Society. UK trademark number
1448790.

A catalogue record for this book is available from the British Library

Printed and bound in the UK, February 2014, LH26

Contents

Passage of Time (2)

Passage of Time (3)

At Rose's request,
this book is dedicated
to those who, like her, have found
that they are dumb.
"Dumbounded!"
she said with an unexpected
giggle.

Foreword

I am honoured to have been asked to write this foreword as *Goodbye Pink Room* is one of the most powerful books I have ever read. It vividly portrays the experiences of one little girl, and through that experience conjures up for all of us the reality of what the label Childhood Sexual Abuse really means.

The unfolding of the Jimmy Savile story; the courage of Frances Andrade who gave compelling and convincing evidence but committed suicide before the guilty verdict was given; the tenacity of the child sexual exploitation victims in Rochdale, Oxford, and elsewhere; all these made 2013 a year when Childhood Sexual Abuse reached into public consciousness as never before. Accounts like this are now needed, to help us understand in more depth some of the challenges in protecting children and in creating the possibility of them speaking out earlier, when protection has failed.

Please don't read this if you want to maintain a glib belief that "These things couldn't happen in my community" or "The people I know are too good to get involved in abuse." But if you want your humanity enlarged, if you want to increase your ability to listen, to see, to understand and to empathize, then you have found a treasure.

Within the Church of England and the Methodist Church, we now give this book to all new Bishops and Chairs of District as part of their safeguarding induction. So I write for the church generally as well as for myself personally, when I thank Jane Grayshon for writing this book, and "Rose" for sharing her story.

Elizabeth Hall
Safeguarding Adviser for the Church of England
and the Methodist Church

Preface

Rose asked me to write her story: a request that made me afraid; awed at the enormity of the task, despite being aware of the immense privilege. It was with considerable trepidation that I accepted. I had witnessed how harrowed Rose became whenever aspects of her childhood were raised in conversation. Ghost-writing was not to be taken lightly and we agreed that supervision was essential for both of us. She was plagued with nightmares even before she began to focus on telling her story to enable me to put it into the public domain.

I was not wholly surprised, therefore, when she seemed troubled rather than pleased on the day I presented her with the finished manuscript. My conscience prickled, especially when she spoke.

"Thank you," she said. I knew her well enough to discern that she was calling upon her determination to muster the courage to speak at all.

She looked down at the bundle of pages as she held the completed manuscript for the first time. As she moved her hand across the top page, I considered the potency of those three words that she was actually stroking. *Goodbye Pink Room.* I winced. How could I have expected her to be pleased when the story she was holding was one of tragedy? "*Goodbye…*": a story in which her childhood innocence had been snatched from her. Yet her way had been to try to say goodbye with dignity. That was closer to her nature than to consider that her childhood had been stolen.

Rose was avoiding eye contact with me: another clue that she was struggling inwardly. I remained silent, unsure of what was troubling her. I had learned by now that kindness would not probe. If I waited, she would have more space in which she might find words – even if only a few staccato ones – to indicate something of the cause of her struggle. Nevertheless, I wanted my presence to be supportive.

My reward came. Rose flashed a quick look at me as if to check that I was listening fully; enough time for me to notice that her eyes had filled with tears.

"This makes my story look so neatly contained," she said.

The pages sat in her hands exactly as I had given them to her: I had taken some pride in tapping them all together, lining up all the edges to make the pile completely straight. "And the thing is, that's exactly what my story *isn't*." Her face had puckered into a frown. "It *isn't* neat, and it *isn't* contained. So how can I cope with it being published? It's as if it's become a lie in the very process of going public."

I shuddered. No wonder I had been nervous about the task of writing her story.

"No, Rose," I said with growing assurance. "This is your own story. We have to let it tell itself in all its simplicity. We have been faithful to you. And the truth simply speaks for itself. It hasn't become a lie."

I ran over the process in my mind… the seemingly endless hours of sitting with her, in all her fragile vulnerability, as she translated misty memories into concrete words. I had not only had to capture Rose's words but also to communicate her cry – a cry with no words. For that reason, the blank pages in this book are as important as the text itself.

There were times when Rose's pain had seemed overwhelming and words had failed her. Occasionally she brought me little drawings. Where I have included these, I have left them to stand on their own. They are *communication*, not *illustration*. They carry more significance than Rose could articulate. Whenever she saw them she wept. For this reason I have honoured them with the gentle cushion of space.

I recollected that when Rose did talk, the manner of her speaking varied. Sometimes her vocabulary was noticeably child-like; at other times she was able to reflect more maturely about her experiences. This I have indicated in italics. She did not tell her story chronologically but in fragments: I have pieced it together, trying to present a sense of her growing up over the years. These are inevitably sketches and not the whole picture, but it's enough. I have changed all names.

So acute is Rose's vulnerability, I have done more than promise to protect her identity. Permission to publish is on the condition that I do not discuss her. It is not Rose whom I am presenting: it is her story in its raw simplicity. Her desire is that others who are unable to speak for themselves might be given some hope by hearing that they are not alone. In fact, she has always wanted to be able to stand *with* her story – not without it – before the God whom she trusts, who loves her (of that she's always been sure), and who nevertheless allowed these terrible things to happen to her.

1

Goodbye Pink Room

Goodbye, pink room.

Goodbye, pink wallpaper that I chose with Granny and Mummy together… when Mummy said that it might be too pink, and Granny said no, because Rose was a lovely pink girl who liked pink things, and the wallpaper would be all right, she said, because there were those white triangles to break it up a little. "And they're so dainty, aren't they?" she twinkled. "Just like Rose herself, who is so dainty."

Was.

Granny said "is" but that's got to be "was" now.

I know that 'cos it isn't dainty for a person to be in a funny position on the ground – not even lying down properly, but sort of perched. Or put into a naughty position in the car. Or have clothes half off – that makes me feel more shy than when he made me take them all right off. At least when they were all off they weren't rucked up or sitting awkwardly or anything.

The daintiness that Granny used to talk about has gone now. And I'm about to go and I'll have to watch more of it go, again, and I'll have that fact pressed into me again…

Aghhh – help, quick, no! No, don't use that phrase, "pressed into" me. I don't like it. I don't LIKE IT! I don't want it; it's horrible, the pressing and pressing and pushing and pressing, in…

"There's room, you know, dear."

No there wasn't! There wasn't room, and don't call me "dear" when you're hurting me! You're HURTING! And I was thinking, before you said there was room, there wasn't any niceness about pressing anything in anywhere.

"Oh, not anywhere, eh? Well, you mean you want me to try somewhere else, do you? You're a mischievous little girl, aren't you? Where else is there a place, where I can press inside?"

No, no, NO! But I must not, shall not, scream or cry, 'cos that would open my mouth and let him in to kiss me all horribly and slobberingly, and I don't WANT him to do that! But I think he's going to come in anyway.

What can I DO?

Mustn't think about that. I'm not there yet. I wonder where I'll be going today. No, I don't want to wonder. Don't want to think. Don't want to go. Don't want him.

Pressing. The word "pressing" is pressing itself in now that I've thought of it. It's almost as bad as when he pressed into me, or tried to, and sometimes didn't manage so he had to go away to "finish it off" on his own, he said. I never dared ask why he went to the bushes, or what it meant to "finish it off". All I knew was what he told me, that he had to do it himself 'cos I wasn't good enough. That's when he got out of the car and made funny groaning noises. He sounded as if he was hurt, but I couldn't dare ask. I just sat where he'd told me, waiting, frozen, unable to move or think.

I must stop myself from thinking now. I'm not there yet. I'm still here, in my pink bedroom. I was saying goodbye before I go.

Goodbye, teddy. Let me touch your fur before I go. Goodbye, fur that's left. It's been rubbed off from so much hugging, and I wish I'd had a nicer, fluffier teddy that had soft bits to feel and stroke. But this teddy has been here forever, and has sat, and watched, and… oh, I wish teddy knew.

Teddy, there's something that is something, but… oh, I can't tell you, and I wish I could, but you mustn't know 'cos this isn't for children so it isn't for you either.

. . . .

I know you're always here, and you are sort of a friend, and I like following my finger along the line of your mouth, and I like stroking the fur on your toes, but there's a secret that I know and you can't share, and I don't like that. I know something that you don't know, and I'm about to find out more about it, and I don't want to. Teddy! I don't want to leave you! I don't want to go!

Goodbye, teddy.

I've got to go, you see.

I hope you'll be here when I get back. Will you be? You will be the same, won't you?

I wonder if I will be the same, too? Or will I have changed? Does something happen to me when he does these things? How will I be when I get back this time? Might my pants be dirty? What will I DO if they are? Will I be able to rub them properly clean? Or if they've got wet, will the wetness leak onto any of my other clothes? What will Mummy say?

Might my cardigan get torn? Might a button come off if he tugs too hard? He's never careful like me.

Will my hair get ruffled by his horrible big hands, when he says he's "caressing" and other big words he uses, but I know that all he's doing is just messing it up?

Teddy, you don't know what happens when I go out like this. I'll be back before tonight, but what will have happened to me by then? What might he have done?

I don't want to go, but I've got to. And it's nearly time.

Next to teddy is my Santa Claus doll. Goodbye, yellow-dress doll with your rustly petticoats that I heard before I saw you. I'm smiling as I remember how I woke up on that very exciting morning. I knew it was Christmas Day but I didn't know if Santa would have come, and if he had, what would he have brought? And then as I moved my legs I heard a crinkly sound and I was puzzled and excited at the same time and didn't know what anything was until I sat straight up in one burst and then I saw you peeping out from the top of my stocking at the end of my bed, and there you were and oh, I felt so, so excited! I knew that Santa Claus had been terribly generous to give me a doll. Mummy and Daddy can't be generous like that 'cos they haven't got enough money; but I don't think that that's all of the reason. I'm not sure, but I think that Santa Claus must understand some things that Mummy and Daddy don't understand. You see, Mummy and Daddy always say that we can be just as happy to have things from our cousins, including my dollies, but I wasn't just as happy. I had always wanted to have a proper doll all of my own. Well, Santa Claus must have known what I thought. I think he must understand girls better than Mummy and Daddy do. I'm the only girl in my family 'cos I've only got brothers, and it's easy to give boys presents 'cos you just give them bits of train set.

I do remember how Mummy smiled nicely when she saw how much I liked you, dolly, but I sometimes get a bit frightened inside myself that if Mummy had a peephole from the kitchen, up through the ceiling into my bedroom above her, and if she could see how much time I spend just combing your hair even when it's already smooth and shiny, I think she'd probably shout upstairs to me, "Rose, you're just wasting time! There are far more important things to do than just fuss around with dolls!" But Santa Claus was different. He had found such a lovely doll for me; one that had petticoats like proper ladies' ones. You have such lovely full, crinkly petticoats.

I like you, doll. Your legs are so fine and beautiful. Your hair is so smooth. Your face has a smile. Your yellow dress is still clean; it still looks lovely.

Will my dress stay clean today? Will I stop being lovely? What will happen to my legs? Oh, no, I mustn't think about that, such a dirty bit. What about my hair? Will it stay smooth, or be rubbed into a mess? Will my lips have a lovely bow shape like yours?

. . . .

GOODBYE PINK ROOM

Or is a lovely bow shape the reason things go wrong?

Does that mean it's my fault?

Your smile, doll… I've always thought that smiles were good, but on some days, like today, I wonder if they might be bad. Some days they seem to be all wrong. Ought I always to smile, no matter what Uncle George says and no matter what he does? Or, when I come home, will I be able to smile when Mummy says, "Say thank you to Uncle George." And, "Say it *nicely*, Rose! What's happened to your face? Come along now, where's your smile?"

One day, if something really bad happens, might it be so bad that I can't manage to keep smiling any longer even if Mummy tells me to?

Might something really bad happen this day, so that I stop being able to smile?

Oh, help, help, what can I do if that happens? No, no, I couldn't bear that to happen. It mustn't. Let me look at your smile, dolly, and I'll try to remember always how to smile like you.

Daddy often says he likes my smile. Only, he says my smile is in my eyes more than my lips 'cos "they twinkle", he says. "Miss Dimples", he calls me sometimes. Or "Miss Twinkles". I feel very skippy when he says things like that.

Oh, if only someone would ask what *had* happened, or why *was* my face not smiling? When Mummy asks things like that on the doorstep when Uncle George brings me home, she doesn't seem to be asking a question, really. At least, I never feel as if she's asking. I only feel as if she's saying her question as a way of telling me off.

Oh dear: I can feel my lips quivering now, 'cos I want to cry, but I know that I mustn't. I mustn't. Only babies cry, and I mustn't be a baby. It's just that I noticed that I almost did – by mistake – but then I was careful and I managed to stop myself. There, it's all right now. See, I don't want to cry really. So I'm not.

• •

I don't want to go. But it's nearly time. Very, very nearly. My wind-up alarm clock inside my heart is tick-tocking, pushing the hands towards the time he'll come and get me.

I wish I'd said "collect" me then, instead of "get" me. But I'd said that he'll "get" me before I had time to think. And that is how it feels. He's coming to get me. His hands will get me.

What can I do to get ready to go? How can I "prepare"?

I'm just touching what's here, in my room: what's mine, and I'm saying goodbye...

Goodbye, desk.

I don't want to go, but I've got to. Soon the doorbell will ring. He'll have arrived. It'll be time for me to go. The "treat" will begin.

So... goodbye, desk. I'm just staring at you now, staring and staring and not moving at all. I'm thinking about how I like learning things, and I love sitting in front of you, and it's nice that you used to be Daddy's desk... but the trouble is, whenever I come home from my treats, I sit down at you and my mind just goes all blank. I try to do my homework and, instead of seeing my spelling lists, all I can see is the car windscreen, or the fields outside, or the bushes where he's gone to do whatever he does there... and I won't have learned the spellings I was supposed to have learned.

I HATE this! I want to work and I can't. I want to smile and I can't. I want to go out to be free, and instead I come home and feel I've been put into prison. And I'm all the more trapped 'cos he says he might tell on me one day. If I'm not a good girl, he says, and if I don't do exactly what he says. He might tell Mummy and Daddy that I've been terribly, terribly naughty, and rude...

That would be so very terrible. Every day, whenever that thought comes to me, I hope and hope that he will never ever tell, but I'm frightened that he might one time. I could never stop him if he did. I do try to be good so he won't, but I don't always manage to be completely good. Oh, I mustn't cry, but what on earth would Mummy and Daddy say if he ever told them about me?

I mustn't cry.

Goodbye, room.

Nice, pink room.

Goodbye, pink room.

I don't want to go. I don't know what to do. Please, don't you change, room. Please be here, and be the same, when I come home. You see, I still want to have a nice, dainty room… a pink room… but what if I've been changed into a girl who's not dainty any more? I'm a bit frightened that I might know the answer already. I think that the real truth is that I can't be called dainty any more – not properly dainty – because of all the things…

I don't want to think that, though, because I want to keep being dainty, and nice, and like my nice pink room. That's why I don't want to say goodbye to it now…

There is my Bible, on the top of the pile: the Bible that says that God cares, and that He is everywhere. Thank You, God, for caring, and extra-thank You because You're my Friend. And please, God, please d'You think You can let me feel You today? If Uncle George laughs at me after he's asked me something and I get the answer wrong even when I've tried to get it right – and if I don't know what's wrong about what I've said or done and he still laughs, please – *please*! – do You think You could possibly let me FEEL where You are? 'Cos I know that You're with us always, so that includes me when Uncle George is laughing at me. And I know that You see everything, and You understand us, and You care. The Bible says so. It's just that when I can't see You or feel You, I get more frightened and sometimes I want to cry from loneliness. Just accidentally cry, that is.

Goodbye, Bible.

But I won't say goodbye to You, God. I want You to stay being with me, like the Bible says.

I don't like saying goodbye.

Back to the Beginning

2

Tea for Two

I've just said "Nerr" to my brother Roger, which isn't kind of me and I feel quite guilty now and inside myself I know I've been nasty. I know I shouldn't have said that and especially I shouldn't have done what I did next, and I'm sorry, Jesus, and thank You for forgiving us when we say sorry when we mean it, which I do. But Roger had been bragging so much about how Oliver *and* Philip *and* Julian had all been to Uncle George's house and now *he* had too, and he sounded as if that made him be so much better than me, and as if he's much more important than me... And I know that they're all much more grown up than me even though I try very hard to be grown up but I never win 'cos they're older, but in the end I really shouted to Roger that "I'VE BEEN TOO", all on my own, and that's when I said the word "Nerr" and then – and I'm very sorry about this, Jesus – then I stuck my tongue out at him.

I shouldn't have stuck my tongue out and as soon as I'd done it, or even while my tongue was still out, I blushed, 'cos I knew it was very naughty of me. But even then Roger still said I'd *never* been, which is when I shouted back, "I HAVE!" and he said, "Haven't!" and then we argued by just saying in turns, "Have!" "Haven't!" And it's not fair 'cos I *have* been and it must've been when Roger was on his Scout camp and that must be how he didn't know about it. And in the end I said that to him, which is when he went away 'cos he could see that I was right and he couldn't argue any more, but the trouble is I expect he'll have gone to tell Mummy that I stuck my tongue out at him and I'm waiting for what'll happen next. I feel a bit frightened in case she gives me a good hiding 'cos it's a rule that we mustn't put our tongues out of our mouths.

Anyway I *did* go to Uncle George's and I *am* growing up and when I was invited to Uncle George's that was like a sort of "sign" of how much I am, and that's very good. And I hope that I might get invited to go again, another time, but I don't know. It's rude to ask, and Mummy says you never invite yourself to anywhere, so I've just got to wait and see.

My brothers have all been for tea there. And I can remember when Roger became old enough to go for the first time, 'cos that wasn't so very long ago. It was when I first moved to the different primary school, I think, the one that's a bit further away than my first school but Mummy and Daddy said that this school would give me a better chance of winning a scholarship to the posh school when I'm eleven. Anyway I remember Roger going for his first time 'cos he bragged so very much about the fact that he was going, and before he went he kept coming into my room and saying lots of times how this proved that he's so much older than me, and he kept on gloating and crowing, and I don't like him. But I know I shouldn't say that, and I'm sorry.

The only good thing is that in Sunday school I remember Daddy once teaching us – he was on the stage in front of all the children together before we went into our separate groups – and Daddy taught all of the big group of us that there's a difference between "like" and "love". He said that we have to love everybody 'cos that's Jesus' command, and the most important of all the Ten Commandments are about love. But he said that we don't have to "like" everybody, because liking is different from loving. And I think that's a good job 'cos I don't like Roger 'cos he's always bragging so much. But Daddy told us to be very careful if you don't like someone, because you have to *find* the love for that

GOODBYE PINK ROOM

person, whereas if you like them you don't have to go looking for the love; it's already there because that's part of liking them.

I quite often think about this for me with Roger, except I know Daddy's right that you have to go looking for the love, and sometimes when I don't like Roger when he's crowing over me and saying things that I don't think are always completely true, then I have to look and look and sometimes I haven't managed to *find* the love which I know is something that makes God be very disappointed in me and I know I've got to ask Him to help me find it. Daddy says that that's a good kind of prayer but it's the kind of prayer that takes a lot of learning, he says, and when I told Daddy I hadn't learned it yet, I thought he'd have some advice, but all he said was that if at first you don't succeed, try, try, and try again. I do keep trying. I'm very glad that Daddy says it's a good kind of prayer if you have to keep looking and if you haven't found the love yet, 'cos I haven't really found it well enough and when Roger's saying a lot of things that I don't like I sort of burn inside myself and I go very hot and I wish he'd go away or at least shut up.

And I didn't like Roger when he came back from Uncle George's 'cos – I remember this so clearly – he wouldn't tell me anything at all about what had happened. I think that was very mean of him 'cos usually when you do something exciting you come back and tell everybody all about it, but he didn't and he wouldn't say anything except, "It's a secret, and it's only for people who are old enough." And that's one time when I got my burning feeling inside myself because of how much I didn't like him.

Anyway, the important thing for now is that now *I* am big enough and grown up enough to go, and Uncle George said so, which is why I said "Nerr". And when Uncle George first invited me during one Sunday tea, which is when he always comes to our house, Mummy and Daddy said they'd need to talk about it, and

I thought that was very embarrassing of them 'cos I think they should either have said, "Oh yes please" or "How delightful!" or else they should have said, "Oh, well, thank you, George..." (they don't have to call him "Uncle"), "...but perhaps not yet." But they didn't say either of those, and I was waiting for the answer, and when Mummy said about "needing to talk about it" I blushed 'cos I felt so embarrassed, but Uncle George said that was fine. I didn't say anything or look at anyone when this happened – I just looked at my hands in my lap – but when Uncle George said it was fine, I did look up. He was looking at me and he made a face behind Mummy's back that sort of mouthed the words, "It's all right." So I believed him and I was very glad that he seemed to understand, and that was the first time I knew I could really trust him.

Anyway, Mummy and Daddy had their Discussion about whether I was allowed to go or not, and they decided that I was allowed, which was very exciting. Daddy explained that this might seem funny to me – funny-peculiar, that is, not funny-ha-ha – but that the reason why they needed to discuss it was because they needed to make sure that I would be safe. And the problem was that they both feel that Forest Lane, where Uncle George lives, might not be very safe, because there are bushes and anyone could hide in those bushes and then jump out at me when I walked past. After Daddy had said that, and he said it in a calm voice, Mummy joined in and her eyes looked very fierce, almost as if I'd done something wrong already even though I hadn't. She repeated what Daddy had just explained, only she made it sound more frightening, the way she said, "These men, they hide in those bushes and you don't see them, and they're up to no good – no good at all – and then they're upon you before you know that they're even *there!*" Then she pulled a face that made her look a bit like Granny with her lips pulled tight together to make a face that we all understand in our family, 'cos it means that she definitely disapproves. You mustn't ever argue with her when she pulls her lips together extra-tightly.

Then Mummy started her speech that she often gives, and I don't know why she says it so many times, and she says, "I get to hear about these matters at work every week – every *week*!" I did what I think I was supposed to do, which was I looked as if I was listening, as if Mummy had never said those things before, although I do know the next words off by heart, which are: "You really have no idea what a wicked world we live in." She looked cross, as if she was blaming me that I don't have any idea, but I do try very hard to have an idea and I did promise that I would be very careful. Then she said that it would be all right as long as I keep my eyes open, which I think is a bit of a silly thing to say. I wouldn't walk along to Uncle George's house with my eyes closed, and especially not down a lane with bushes where there might be a bad man hiding who could leap out at me any time.

Daddy said that he thought it was reasonable for me to go to Uncle George's because we must bear in mind that it wasn't so very different from normal, seeing as how I walk past the end of his lane every day on the way home from school. He said that Rose had always been very sensible, and when he said that, I felt all warm inside, and I was glad Daddy was in on the Discussion. He said that Rose had proved that she had a good head on those shoulders of hers and also that she's demonstrated some good, sound, common sense and he meant things like always keeping to the opposite side of the road when walking past the end of Forest Lane so I keep well clear of those bushes. Therefore, he said, the point now was that there is only one brief moment of danger if I'm to go to Uncle George's house on my own, and that is the walk from the beginning of Forest Lane up to Uncle George's actual house. Since Uncle George lives at number 10, there are only four houses' worth of dangerous lane for me to go past, 'cos the houses go 2-4-6-8 and then number 10 is his house.

Therefore, he said, we must get a sense of proportion (I think he meant Mummy and himself, really, but I didn't say that, of course) and that it would be all right for me to go, because Rose could certainly be trusted to be aware of the danger. And he gave me a twinkle of his eye at the end that was almost a smile, but not quite, and he said quietly, "Forewarned is forearmed, dear." I smiled back to him, and I just said, "Yes."

He and Mummy began to leave my room 'cos that was the end of the Conference, but before Mummy kissed me goodnight she said, "Well, be forewarned!" in a way that nearly made me feel a little bit frightened again, but Daddy was still beaming when he bent forward to kiss me on my forehead and he tucked my blankets around my shoulders very snugly so I stayed feeling safe, all tucked up in bed, and when they'd left my room and before I went to sleep I got very excited about growing up and I was thinking about going to Uncle George's.

On another day, when Daddy and I were on our own, Daddy explained to me that the reason these things are important is that I'm so precious, and that he and Mummy wouldn't want anything to happen to me. And he said that it may all sound like quite a fuss, but in fact my safety is very important to him and Mummy because they love me so much, and "Of course, you are my Darling Daughter!" Daddy often says that last bit – maybe he even says it most days – so when he said, "You are my…" I knew what the next two words were. He took the special kind of breath that he does before he says those words, and he waited until I looked back at him, and after he'd taken his breath I joined in with him so that I said the last two words *with* him. So we both finished his sentence together, in a loud voice – "Darling Daughter!" – that sounded a little bit as if we were singing together. And then we kept looking at one another while we both laughed and I felt very happy.

I'm very lucky to have parents who love me so much and who care for me so much and who take so much trouble to make sure I don't get into danger, and I think it's a good thing that they make me be prepared and that makes me be safe from bad people, like someone who might be lurking in bushes in Forest Lane. Daddy's right that I *have* learned how to be very watchful and I *do* know how to stay alert and that's why, whenever I walk past the end of Forest Lane with its dangerous bushes, I make sure I'm very alert and I feel a little bit important, too, 'cos I know I'm being so careful to keep safe.

So after the Discussion, I was excited all week looking forward to going to Uncle George's house for tea, especially 'cos I was going all on my own, without my brothers. Uncle George has a housekeeper, which means the same as having a maid, I think, only she lives there all the time. Anyway, Daddy said that Priscilla's presence made the whole arrangement secure and proper. I'm not completely sure why he said that and I didn't want to ask in case that would have caused Mummy to give another speech. But I think the reason why he said "secure" was that Priscilla must be the person who makes sure that the door is closed securely, 'cos I do know she always opens the door to visitors and she always sees them out, too. So that must be why she makes things secure, if she closes the door properly and locks it as well to make it completely secure. And I think she will make the tea be more "proper" 'cos Uncle George is a bachelor (which means he's never got married, which is why our family feels quite sorry for him), and he can't make tea properly or do baking and the housekeeper always does it for him.

On the day I went to Uncle George's house, I was looking forward to it all day in school, and I told William who sits next to me in our class but he can't have realized how exciting it was for me 'cos he just said, "Oh." I was a bit disappointed about that. However, after school I ran down Hill Street, which is a very steep hill and I love running down it, and I turned into Bridge Road and slowed down so I knew I was being careful before I came to

Forest Lane where I was very, very careful indeed and I stayed as close to the houses as I could so that I kept as far away from the bushes as possible, but also I checked any bushes so I knew that there wasn't anybody behind any of them. I knew I was being very safe, and I knew Daddy would have been very proud of me.

When I got to number 10 I had to stand on my tip-toes to reach 'cos the bell was so high up on the wall by Uncle George's front door, and it was a big fat rounded button that bulged out of a big circle of brass that I think Priscilla must polish every day 'cos it was as shiny as a mirror.

When Priscilla came to the door I thought she'd be very friendly, but she wasn't and she didn't really look at me properly. When she spoke, she didn't open her mouth very far so I couldn't hear the words very clearly, which made me feel shy 'cos I didn't want to keep saying, "Pardon?" Granny says we should enunciate well but Priscilla didn't do that.

Anyway she must have been expecting me 'cos as soon as she opened the door she said, "Come in", in a very low voice that sounded flat and unexcited and almost as if she didn't want me to be there, which didn't seem to be very friendly of her. When I did step in I saw that the hall was gloomy with just one light bulb hanging without a proper lampshade, so when she closed the front door everywhere became so dim that suddenly I didn't like it very much. I could only just make out the chair where she told me to put my leather satchel and my school gabardine.

Then she muttered something else that I couldn't hear exactly, but she opened another door so I followed her, and that's where Uncle George was and he began to stand up when I went in and he held out his hand welcomingly to say hello to me. As soon as I'd walked into the room properly, Priscilla began to close the door behind me and Uncle George called after her, "Yes, tea straight away please, P." I thought he must be very special and very important to have a maid, just like the Queen has, and I felt very important being in Uncle George's house with a maid opening and closing the door for me.

Then Uncle George let me choose which chair I'd like, and I chose the one opposite his, on the other side of the big open fireplace, which was stacked up high with coal underneath and a big log crackling away on the top like a cairn on the top of a mountain. It was very cosy in Uncle George's drawing room and there were lots of big pictures in patterned gold frames that reflected the sparkling, dancing flames from the fireplace.

I think Uncle George must be very rich to have a maid and all those big pictures and lots of leather books in such beautifully polished dark wooden bookshelves, and he had one bookshelf in one corner of the room that turned round, like the globe we have in our classroom, only this was huge and it didn't have a map on 'cos it was full of books instead. Uncle George told me that that's called a Revolving Bookcase and he let me push it round, very carefully of course, so that I could see the spines of the different books and the gold lettering on them, and when I pushed it the Revolving Bookcase squeaked and I thought it was as if it was singing a song about all the stories contained in all those books.

Priscilla came back in almost immediately, so she must've had our tea all prepared and ready before I'd pressed the doorbell. But when she came in she still didn't talk to me and she didn't smile either, even though she was pushing a trolley that looked so wonderful. I don't know how she could have brought it in without bursting with pleasure at all the loveliness she was pushing in front of her.

There was a pretty embroidered tray-cloth on each shelf, although the flowers didn't quite match 'cos one was tulips and the other was roses, but that didn't matter. On the top shelf she'd laid out our cups and saucers, the matching plates, and little napkins held down by miniature knives and forks, and also there were little bowls of jam and butter and cream for our scones. The little milk-jug, the sugar bowl, and the teapot were all silver and they'd been polished just like the brass circle around the doorbell, and the teapot was big enough for you to see the reflection of the whole of Priscilla with her white apron, only it made her look fat, which she wasn't.

On the bottom shelf of the trolley there were big plates with scones, and sandwiches with no crusts on (Mummy says we've got to eat the crusts but with Priscilla's tea I didn't have to!), and there were biscuits that weren't just plain digestives: they had chocolate on the top in a pattern with wiggly lines all the way across them. And finally there was a cake stand with two tiers, a little bit like a double-decker bus, with one big round cake with white icing on the top tier, and on the lower tier were four brandy snaps with cream oozing out of either end.

I'd never seen such a huge tea and I felt very excited inside myself and I said "Ooh, thank you *very* much," and I'm sure Priscilla must've known from my voice that I was really happy, but she just grunted and I just don't know why. And when she handed me my cup she still didn't smile to me, even though I smiled to her, but she didn't even look at me properly and instead she went back to the trolley and she seemed to need to concentrate on looking at Uncle George's teacup. So altogether she didn't look at my face at all, which I think is a bit odd 'cos it was almost as if she didn't want to see me, or as if she didn't want to know who I was.

As soon as she'd passed Uncle George his teacup, she pointed her arm towards the bottom of the trolley and she muttered something which must have meant, "Do help yourself", but she didn't offer any of the food round like I do on a Sunday when Uncle George comes to our house when I've done the baking. And she left the room 'cos Uncle George said, "That'll be all, thank you P." I think he must call her "P" for short, instead of saying Priscilla.

· ·

GOODBYE PINK ROOM

I don't drink tea at home. I have milk after school, but I didn't say that to Priscilla or to Uncle George 'cos I wanted to show how grown up I can be. So I put two lumps of sugar in 'cos Philip says that makes tea taste better, and I managed to drink it all, so that meant I was polite. And anyway the sandwiches and scones and cake and biscuits were all really scrummy, which is my word for a mixture of "scrumptious" and "yummy", which is what they were.

I knew before I even went to Uncle George's house that he was friendly and understanding, especially from that sign he gave when he'd invited me and when he mouthed behind Mummy's back, "It's all right." But while we were having our tea he helped me to know that even more, 'cos he actually said that he wanted to be a special friend to me, which was very kind of him, especially when he was such an important man as I was beginning to see from his grand style of living with a housekeeper. And he said he understood things, for example about Mummy being very strict, and I was surprised when he said that about Mummy 'cos nobody had ever dared to say anything like that about Mummy. But Uncle George did dare, and then he asked me if I was shocked to hear him saying that, and I wasn't sure what to say to him 'cos I *was* shocked but also a little bit of me felt quite glad.

Then, just when I wasn't quite sure what to say or how to answer him, he said, "Rose?" in a way that caused me to look at him and I saw his face, and he smiled to me with an extra kind smile which told me I didn't need to say any words, 'cos what was important was that he understood. At that moment I knew I could trust him more than ever, 'cos suddenly I could feel the niceness of somebody being so understanding of what it's like being in my family. I'd never heard anybody ever say anything about my Mummy being strict, but Uncle George did on that day and that was very nice of him.

He was even more thoughtful because he said he'd been thinking about me and he'd decided that it must be hard for me because I'm a very faithful girl, he said, so that's how he knew I wouldn't ever be rude about Mummy, and he said that I must've learned well about not talking behind somebody's back, and was that in Sunday school? And I said, "Yes." So then he said that seeing as I wouldn't say bad things (I didn't tell him that I'd ever said "Nerr" to Roger), then he would be a good friend to me. He said that because he's a grown-up, he can say some things that are true, but children aren't allowed to say them. He said that he'd like to be a friend to me in this way, so I didn't have to struggle with secrets all on my own because, he said, it is actually a *fact* that my Mummy is very strict.

I was very surprised at him saying all this, but I did know that what he said was true, just a little bit anyway. So the next thing was that we both giggled 'cos we both know that that's quite naughty to say what he said, but I decided that it proved how very understanding Uncle George must be, and how kind and thoughtful.

When he giggled with me, I began to giggle a little bit more although I was eating my scone at the same time, but I tried not to make crumbs go everywhere, and he said he'd noticed that Mummy can get cross for not-very-much-reason, which made me giggle quite a lot, 'cos nobody *ever* says that sort of thing out loud and I knew he was being naughty.

Then he said, "For example, what *would* your mother say if she saw you now, eh?" Suddenly I felt caught, 'cos I was giggling even though I still had some scone in my mouth, and you're not allowed to laugh; you have to only smile until your mouth is empty. But when Uncle George said that, he made me giggle such a lot by then, and he was chuckling too only he didn't have his mouth full, and I dropped a crumb and he opened his eyes very wide as if I had done a Terrible Sin, except he wasn't glaring but chuckling. Then I began to get the giggles completely at his funny face, which made us both laugh more and more. He didn't

GOODBYE PINK ROOM

tell me off or tell me to "Stop that right *now*, my girl!" which showed me that he must have known that it was nice to have fun, and I decided he was very considerate. Granny says that a considerate person is someone who can imagine another person's situation, which is a very good attribute. Granny often uses the word "attribute".

So that was how I knew for certain that Uncle George really is very considerate. Altogether he was very reassuring to me and it was very nice when I went to his house for tea. Because also I learned that Uncle George is very understanding about what it's like to be *me!* Especially when he said he knows that I'm a good girl and that I'm very faithful and he said how much I care about what God thinks. Uncle George is right 'cos I *do* care and I *do* want God to be pleased with me and Jesus *is* my Friend 'cos I talk to Him a lot. So I was very happy when Uncle George said he'd noticed that about me, and I felt all glowing inside. And Uncle George really helped me not to feel guilty when I wish Mummy wasn't so strict, 'cos he helped me by saying words for me that I wouldn't say, so he said I don't need to feel bad, and the important thing from this tea time was for me to remember that *he understands me* and *he wants to be as good a friend as he possibly can be.*

I don't know how he understood so much but I was very glad he was so understanding. That's when he came up with the solution that everything would be completely safe as long as we keep what we'd said as our secret, which I know it would have to be 'cos we couldn't say things like that to Mummy, and we couldn't giggle and make crumbs in front of Mummy or what would she say? Which is completely true. He promised that he'd never tell on me that I'd said to him that Mummy is strict. And he said that everything was all right – we could have some secrets – and then he said that he knows other things that Mummy doesn't know and he promised he'd tell me things as I grow to be big enough, which is very exciting.

. . . .

I don't know when Uncle George will tell me more things but I can't wait.

In the meantime, I think – I'm not quite sure – but I think that Uncle George might also be able to understand if I said to him that I said "Nerr" to Roger. He might help me to feel forgiven, 'cos if I tell him how much my brothers tease me and how they don't believe what I say, he might understand. I hope he might. And I hope that he'll maybe understand why I stuck my tongue out at Roger, too, and if Mummy does smack me or if she gets Daddy to put me over his knee to give me a good hiding then I'll be able to think, while it's all happening, that I hope I'll be able to see Uncle George on his own again. If I can, then I'll be able to tell him and he'll understand, and that'll help me to feel a bit less terrible 'cos he helped me so much when I went for tea.

But first I'll have to be sure that Uncle George can keep secrets 'cos I would get into terrible trouble if anybody found out that I'd been talking about Mummy behind her back. Actually I already feel very sad about that, and guilty, so I really hope he will keep the secret.

Uncle George did promise that he wouldn't tell. And he is a teacher at a big school, and he is very important in our church, and those two things mean that everyone should trust him. That must be why everyone does trust him. So that means that I shall try to trust him, too.

3

Sunday Tea

I'm looking quite proudly at the butterballs that I made very early this morning before church. I made them before Mummy and Daddy even got out of bed, 'cos when I'd woken up I'd had an idea for Uncle George coming for tea. Uncle George comes for tea almost every Sunday, but this Sunday I'm extra-excited because of my idea. I'm really hoping that he might ask who made the butterballs, 'cos then he'll find out that it was me and then he'll be pleased with me.

All the butterballs are sitting in their little glass dish and we have a very teeny tiny knife that's called a butter knife but I sometimes use it when I'm playing with my crinkly-petticoat dolly 'cos I think it's the right size for a doll. Anyway the little knife is perching on the edge of the glass dish, ready for the first person to pick up a butterball, which I hope will be Uncle George.

I'm very pleased that I managed to get almost all of the balls to be very round, and not too wobbly which is how they used to look when I first made them when I was younger. It's very hard to get them completely round 'cos if you don't get it right on your first try, the butter starts to stick on the wooden bats that you use to make them with. But last time Granny was at our house, she told me that her secret is to make sure the butter bats have soaked in water for long enough before you start. That's why I put them in a jug of water last night before I went to bed, so that they had all night to soak and get so that the butter wouldn't stick to them. And I think that has helped me, and the butter didn't get too stuck this morning, and I'm glad I made them when nobody else was in the kitchen 'cos nobody was there to tell me I was taking too long, and anyway I got to lick the butter bats at the end myself without having to give them to one of my brothers.

I've felt very excited all the time I've been in the kitchen today. Sometimes when I help Mummy to do the baking I feel a bit frightened in case I get in Mummy's way, or if I don't do it quite right and she makes a sound with her tongue that goes "Tut!" and I know she's cross even if she doesn't say any proper words. At least, she's not cross, exactly, but I can feel inside myself that I haven't done things quite right, and then I feel horrible inside 'cos I know I'm not good enough. But today that didn't happen and I didn't make her cross like that and today I did all of the baking, which I help her to do most Sundays but *this* day I haven't only helped her – I've done it all. I've done extra-nice things today so that Uncle George will like them more. And if he does like them more, and if he asks who's been doing all this delicious baking, then someone will tell him that Rose did it, and then he might remember that I felt really happy when I came for tea at his house, and I hope he does remember that 'cos I'd really like to go out as a treat with him which is one thing he said might happen, if I'm very good. That's what I'm hoping about while I wait for Uncle George to need a butterball.

There's only one problem about what he said, which is that, when he said it, he only said "sometime", which is a bit of a pity 'cos that usually means that people will forget. And for lots of Sundays since I went to his house for tea, Uncle George has forgotten, or at least he hasn't said anything. That's why I'm hoping that this might be the Sunday that he'll remember, 'cos I would feel so special if I'm good enough for him to ask me to come on a treat outing. I've watched the films he's shown us of the nice places he goes to and I'd love to go to those sorts of places, especially to the seaside or the countryside. And if he takes me on my own then that will be even better 'cos my brothers will see that I'm old enough to get taken out all on my own with Uncle George, and they'll have to stop saying things about me being too young for everything. And that will make me be special.

I've already given Uncle George his plate and his little knife, but it's not time for me to hand round the cakes 'cos Mummy whispered not yet. So that's why I'm waiting. It's polite to wait until each person has a cup of tea before we take any food on our plates, and she hasn't finished pouring the tea (which I made and carried through, and Uncle George smiled at me when I came through the door and I hoped that that was 'cos he was thinking that I was being helpful).

I can tell that Sunday tea is a special time 'cos this is the only time that we use the special tea-knives. I like these knives because of their beautiful handles. I don't know what the name is for what they're made of, but they are white and they are a little bit shiny just like pearls. They're dainty and I like dainty things. We always use them for Sunday tea with Uncle George just as if we use them every day, but he doesn't know that they're actually specially for Sundays. I think maybe, just maybe, Mummy and Daddy might want to show Uncle George that they've got special things, even though we haven't got a housekeeper.

Anyway, I can't wait for tea to start properly 'cos I made more things and they're all on plates near to the butterballs and I can see everything. I didn't only bake the usual fairy cakes but I also made them to be extra-pretty with icing *and* I found some little pink bits that I sprinkled on top to make them dainty. And there's also the shortbread that I made and I was very careful to make a pattern round the outside by pinching the pastry between my thumb and forefinger, and I made it very small. When Mummy does it the pattern is always big, and sometimes I make the pattern be as big as that but sometimes I can make the pinches closer together, and smaller, which is daintier, and that's what I did earlier this afternoon and I'm admiring how the pattern looks nicer than usual because it's daintier.

Next to the shortbread there are the final things I baked on my own: the "cornflake-chocolate goodies", which is my name for them and I think it's their proper name even though William at school says they're not called that. He says they're called "rice-crispy cakes" and you don't need to say "chocolate". And he says I'm wrong because they're supposed to be made with rice crispies and not cornflakes, but I don't believe him 'cos Granny makes them with cornflakes and she knows. And also, I've seen cornflake ones at the bakery and I've never seen rice-crispy ones… well, except at Ruth's house. And actually I really like the ones that Ruth's mother makes, and they're very different from our ones and once, when I'd been to Ruth's house for tea, I asked Mummy why those chocolatey cakes tasted different from the ones at our house. Mummy just said that they'll be "some complicated recipe" and it's no wonder, because Ruth's mother has time to bake bread and cakes because she doesn't go out to work like Mummy does. And I didn't dare tell Mummy that I liked Ruth's mother's chocolate crispy cakes more than I like our ones, but I've decided that when I grow up I'm going to bake really nice ones for *my* children, even if the recipe is complicated, 'cos they're so scrummy.

One time when I said "Thank you very much" to Ruth's mother for her cakes 'cos I liked them so much (I didn't say I liked them better than Mummy's), she told me that they have syrup and butter. She patted me on the head and said that these were her secret ingredients. She must have secrets like my Granny. Maybe everybody has secrets.

Mummy's only got one more cup of tea to pour out now, and then it'll be time for me to hand round the bread and then the butterballs and the jam. I'm not going to say that it was me who made the butterballs. I can't wait to see if he asks but I really hope he will. 'Cos that's better 'cos he'll just ask, and he'll find out sort of accidentally, and then I really hope he'll think I'm a good girl – good enough for him to invite on a special treat.

And then he might remember his promise for "some day". I am so excited 'cos I really hope that today it just might become real. He might make it "one day soon".

I can't wait to be so grown up 'cos then my brothers won't be the only special ones any longer. I can't wait for that.

4

The First Outing

Uncle George's car has just reached some traffic lights and they've just changed from amber to red, which is why Uncle George had to stop. And while the car's stopped I'm thinking a little bit and I'm watching for them to go green again. Actually I know that they go red-and-amber first, 'cos Daddy often tests me on how traffic lights change colour, and he says it's a bit of a trick question 'cos he told me that most people say that they go "red, amber, green", and they don't notice that it's not actually amber: it's red-and-amber. He's very pleased with me for having learned so well because he says it's hard to catch me out nowadays when he tests me. And what he says is important to remember is that before a traffic light shows green, its red light is *still shining* and *still giving a message*. I know that now. Daddy's also taught me that on the way back up, the traffic lights go "green, amber, red", and he asks me what amber means and he says that *that*'s a bit of a trick question too, 'cos most people say it means "get ready to stop" but it doesn't; it means stop. That's important 'cos you have to put the brakes on before you think it's really necessary, and that's why it's important to learn the signs of when to stop even if you don't think you need to.

So that's why Uncle George had to stop in his car, and I'm thinking quite a lot now that he has.

It's very quiet in the car at the moment 'cos Uncle George isn't talking any more, and neither am I. We're both being silent, which is a bit funny (funny-peculiar, that is) 'cos for the whole of the rest of this afternoon in the car, we've been talking. I didn't mean funny-ha-ha 'cos I don't feel laugh-y or giggly or skippy, which is different from what I thought I would feel when I came out with him on such a treat. I'm not trying to be ungrateful, because I know how important it is to be grateful; it's just that I don't really want to say anything to Uncle George at the moment 'cos I don't know what to say any more, and I'm thinking quite a lot about some things that he said earlier on, on our way *to* the countryside.

At least, I sort of am thinking about what he said, and I sort of don't want to at the same time.

I can hear the car engine, which Oliver says is a very quiet engine although I don't really think it is 'cos I can hear it now, and I think it makes quite a loud noise whenever Uncle George starts off, which he's going to do as soon as the light changes to green. But Oliver says I don't know very much about car engines and actually that's true, and he's right – this time he is – and that's 'cos I don't think car engines are very interesting. I don't get car magazines like Oliver does, when he's saved up his pocket money, although he hides those magazines from Mummy because she says they're just a waste of good money.

I haven't told Mummy that Oliver buys car magazines sometimes, 'cos Oliver would feel sad if I did, and 'cos I think he should be allowed to save up especially 'cos he never ever buys sweets for himself, just so he can get his magazine that he likes so much. And he can't get those magazines very often – not as often as he'd like to, and definitely not every month, which proper collectors do – 'cos it takes him so long to save up for each one. So I think it would be mean for me to tell on him, and that's why I'm keeping that secret 'cos that's a kind thing to do.

Anyway if I did tell, and if any of my brothers found out – Oliver or Philip or Julian or Roger – then they'd wait until Mummy had gone out and then they'd all get together and come and find me, probably in my bedroom, and they'd all start chanting very loudly at me. We always chant to one another if someone has told on anyone else, and it's all right if you're the one chanting but it's horrible if you're the one who has to hear it. If it's me, I nearly cry or sometimes I do cry even though I try to hide it. I get very frightened about this in case they ever saw me crying, 'cos I think that they might call me a sissy, which is something that I would really, really hate. I don't ever want to be called a sissy and I try terribly hard never to be one. But if I cry I know I am one. Which I hate.

If they did the chanting in my bedroom there wouldn't be anywhere else that I could go to get away from them, and I hate the way everyone shouts things in my bedroom 'cos the shouting makes the room start to feel a horrible place instead of my nice, pink room. There are only three words to our chant, and they are, "Tell Tale Tit!", which we sort of sing together but it's not nice singing. It's more like a sort of shout, and we shout it over and over again. I don't know why I giggle when I'm chanting it to the others, 'cos as soon as I'm on my own again, I know that I have been not nice 'cos I can feel not nice inside myself. I don't know why I get to be not nice like that. I wish I didn't shout it with them and I'm sad and I whisper to God that I'm very sorry 'cos it makes me be not a nice girl.

So that's another reason why I won't tell on Oliver about how he saves up for car magazines, 'cos I don't want them singing at me, "Tell Tale Tit!"

Actually, all of a sudden, I've gone all shivery as if I'm cold. My body just gave a little shudder, although it must only have been inside me 'cos Uncle George didn't notice, which is a very big relief. But, oh dear, I really wish I hadn't thought about that chant. It's made me hear a word at the end that I completely don't want to think about, and I feel all prickly and horrible and terribly uncomfortable and I wish I wasn't trapped in the car with

Uncle George. Oh dear: that's a terrible thing for me to have thought to myself in the middle of a treat – that I wish I wasn't trapped in the car with Uncle George – but the trouble is, it's true. Suddenly I wish we were home and I don't know what to do now.

I wish the traffic lights would hurry up and change so that the car would start moving and then maybe I could look out of the window at other things that we pass, and then that would help me to stop thinking about all this horribleness. Oh, help, help!

Hurry up, traffic lights! I want Uncle George to GO again, and I don't like this waiting and waiting until something else might happen before I can get out!

I mustn't cry.

No. It's all right. I won't cry. What I'll do is, I'll sort everything out by explaining it to myself, and that'll help me not to cry.

I just swallowed, ready to explain, sort of inside myself.

The only thing that's happened is that I've noticed something that I hadn't ever noticed before, but it's terrible 'cos when I just thought about that chant inside myself now, I've just realized… the last word…

… Oh, I wish the thing that's happened, *hadn't* happened… because I think it's rude, and I don't know what to do next. Because this word isn't dainty – not at all dainty – in fact it's not nice, but the trouble is that Uncle George said the word earlier…

… I've just swallowed again…

I'm going to try to explain this calmly. Keep calm, Rose. (That's what Daddy would say if I were in the middle of telling him something and I started to get a bit flustered. "Flustered" is something he says I get, but when he says it, his eyes twinkle and I don't feel horrible. I just feel he understands how I'm feeling.)

Of course I couldn't tell Daddy about this 'cos… well, I couldn't. Finish. (That's what Daddy sometimes says: "I didn't. Finish." And when he says that, it means that Mummy can't argue with him any more, or she has to stop accusing him of things, like if she keeps going on and on that he "nearly spilled his drink all down him", she has to stop 'cos he just says, "Well I didn't. Finish." And then everybody is silent, except sometimes we children giggle a little bit, 'cos I think it's funny when Daddy wins an argument like that.)

I'm calmer now. I'm going to explain calmly.

I didn't say the word. It was only Uncle George who said it. And I'm not quite sure why he did, and I can't even remember his whole sentence now, except… oh yes, I remember now. That's right. Uncle George asked me – absolutely suddenly, from nowhere at all, just in the middle of us having a lovely conversation about growing up – he asked me if I was…

… if I was growing up.

At least, those weren't his words. What Uncle George actually said was, "And are you beginning to get some…?" (I don't want to say his word, although he said I ought to 'cos he said that this is all part of growing up.)

And I got such a surprise, it was as if I didn't hear his question properly, 'cos the only thing that was ringing round and round in my head was that last word. Then as it went round and round, I could hear the question mark in the word – oh dear, I must practise saying it so I can be grown up – all right, I can hear the question mark when he said, "Are you beginning to get some… (here is the word) … tits?"

Suddenly, while I was still in the middle of feeling shocked, I realized that he'd asked a question, which meant that I had to answer. But I got all confused 'cos I was wondering how on earth did Uncle George just say such a rude word? So I couldn't work out what his question *was*, so I didn't know how to answer him. But then I realized that I must answer him, so I said "Pardon?" and then he said the whole question again. I've forgotten now exactly what I said as a reply, 'cos I didn't want to say "No", 'cos that would have made him think that I'm just a little girl, which is what Oliver and Philip and Julian and Roger are always teasing me about, and I didn't want Uncle George to tease me as well or to laugh at me, especially 'cos I want to be growing up and I want to be old enough to have been invited out on a treat with him.

I *wish* Uncle George hadn't asked me that question.

I mustn't get tangled up with wishing things that can't happen. So I'm going to believe that actually it was all right – in fact, everything was all right – 'cos I *did* manage to answer and I *did* manage to stay calm and I think I must have behaved like a real, grown-up lady and not just a girl. So that means that Uncle George will be pleased with me, 'cos although I don't remember everything he said, I do remember one thing. I do remember that he said it's very important for a girl to become a lady. Then he promised he'd help me to do that. That means that everything will become all right.

I haven't got bosoms and my chest is still completely flat and Mummy doesn't understand at all because she says girls are much too advanced these days and we don't even have to mention these things until I'm at Big School.

Even though I'm going to believe that it's all right, I still wish inside myself that Uncle George hadn't asked me about mine. I haven't got any.

But never mind! If I keep remembering that it was all right in the end – that everything was all right, and here I am, having a wonderful treat outing – then I won't have to tell myself to keep calm. I shall *be* calm. Which is what Daddy is, and what he says Mummy needs to be whenever she gets into a tizz-wazz, which is his word for when Mummy stops being calm.

I'm back being calm now.

While we've been waiting at these traffic lights, once or twice Uncle George has made the engine go louder with a kind of "broom, broom" sound, and I think he does that when his foot goes "tap, tap" on the accelerator pedal. I think he thinks that makes him sound as if he's a posh racing driver, and maybe if I was in a funny-ha-ha mood I might giggle with him, like I giggle with Daddy about some things when I'm in a skippy sort of mood. But I don't feel giggly or skippy, and what I'm thinking is that when Uncle George taps his foot, it seems as if he doesn't want to have to wait 'cos he'd much rather get going again and he's a bit impatient for the traffic light to go to green again. I think.

I thought that I would feel so happy when I came on this special outing with Uncle George, that I would feel skippy and giggly. I wish I was. I hope I haven't done something wrong.

I hope Uncle George doesn't want to be rushing away from *me*; I mean, I hope he hasn't decided that I've not been good enough. And now that thought has started, I've suddenly begun to get worried again. Maybe the reason he's rushing a little bit and he doesn't want to wait at the traffic lights is 'cos he hasn't had a nice enough time with me? Maybe I haven't been good enough company? Or maybe he's feeling a bit like how Mummy feels when she makes her "tut" sound when I've done something not well enough?

I wish I could do better, when I've tried my very hardest and it's not good enough. I hate that feeling, especially when I've been so excited beforehand – like before today – and when I've expected that the other person would be really pleased with me and they'd say, "Oh, Rose, you are a darling!" I feel all warm inside when anyone says that, like Mummy if I've given her a lovely surprise. Or maybe at school the teacher will write "10/10. Well done!", which doesn't often happen except after spelling tests, which I like. But if I've hoped that it would happen and then it doesn't, I get terribly disappointed. I think that's what I'm feeling right now except I'm sure I mustn't say I'm feeling disappointed, especially when I know this is a very, very big treat for me to be grown up enough to come out on an outing with Uncle George...

... and those two words are a very important part of this outing: "grown up". Uncle George has been very, very kind to me – which I know he always is. And the way he's been kind to me this day is that he said to me – much earlier this afternoon and before we started coming home – he said that he understands that I will want to become a nice grown up when I'm bigger. I'm not sure how he could know that, except that I know he's very kind anyway and everyone says so. But he said that he would be able to help me to become more and more grown up, which made me feel so excited that my whole tummy felt as if it had snakes inside it curling and coiling around and I could feel them moving. (Not real snakes!)

When he'd said that, Uncle George asked me if I wanted to become more grown up, and I said yes, of course! 'Cos I'd love to be able to catch up with my bigger brothers and anyway I know that God wants us to become "mature", which is a posh word for "more grown up". I want to be whatever God wants, 'cos I know inside myself how much happier I feel every time I think about what God wants and that makes God happy and I like making Him be happy. I like the fact that in the Bible Jesus said that He doesn't even want us to "serve" Him (which is what I've always thought), but last week when I was reading my Bible, which I do every night before I go to sleep, I found that Jesus said that He wants us to be His friends. I keep thinking how lovely that is, and I think that's one of the best things Jesus said, and I really like imagining myself being Jesus' friend. That way, I feel very special, and I want to feel special.

Aha! The traffic light has just changed to red-and-amber, which means "Get Ready", and any moment it's going to change... yes, *now!* Green. Green for "Go". Uncle George has begun to go, and this is when I think the engine is making a noise even though Oliver says it's a very quiet engine.

I can still keep thinking while we're driving along. I don't have to stop thinking just 'cos Uncle George is doing something, like taking me back from the lovely countryside that he took me to.

What I was thinking was about becoming more grown up.

Mummy and Daddy have never given me a special lesson about growing up and until today I had never noticed before that they weren't helping me grow up. But when Uncle George was being very understanding about them, he guessed that they hadn't helped me, and he asked me if I knew some things – which I didn't – and then he explained to me that they hadn't taught me some important things. That made me feel puzzled, because I thought that they had been teaching me everything, but Uncle George showed me that they can't be. But he said that he would make everything become all right, because he would be able to explain things to me and to show me some things and that would all help me to become grown up.

There is just one other thing about this afternoon, and I think it happened next after Uncle George had asked about... I don't want to say the word!... although I'm not completely sure 'cos everything has become a bit blurry. What I do remember is that after he'd said the first naughty word, then he said another word, which is something that I think is terribly rude. But I'm very confused 'cos the trouble is, when he said it – and this thing was just one word – when he said the word, Uncle George looked at me straight away.

I think he must have been looking at my face so that he could tell what I was thinking. I wanted so much to show Uncle George that I am getting to be a grown-up; I didn't want to show on my face what I really felt inside myself, which was that I felt very shocked to hear him say that word. 'Cos I think – no, I used to think, until Uncle George talked to me today about growing up – I *used* to think that that word was only for older people. But with Uncle George I did manage to be quick enough to make sure that I didn't let my face look shocked on the outside. I managed to make my face look just blank, as if he hadn't said something "different", or something that I wouldn't say. I realized that if I am going to be a grown-up then I should talk in a grown-up way, and if I didn't do that before today's outing (which I didn't, 'cos I haven't ever used that word), I'll need to pretend to Uncle George that I do talk like that, and I do use that word, and then he'll see that I'm growing up.

That's why I tried very, very hard to keep my face exactly the same. I think that Uncle George believed me 'cos he then used the same word again. I didn't really like that, 'cos the trouble is that it's a word that says…

… It's a word that…

… I don't like this word, and I don't want to say it myself, and fortunately I didn't have to say it back to Uncle George, which is a relief 'cos I wouldn't want to say it, but I wish I hadn't had to listen to him saying it so many times. The thing is that it's a word that sometimes – only *some* times, about two or three times ever in my life – I've heard Roger saying to Philip, and they've both giggled, and it's a word that's about what boys have for spending a penny with, and girls don't have one. So of course when Roger and Philip are giggling or when they use that word I feel very left out. But when Uncle George said it, I wasn't left out 'cos Uncle George was saying it to me, and I could tell that he was talking in a way that expected me to understand all about what that thing does.

When he'd said the word the second time, after he'd looked at me, I remember that he said, "I bet you didn't know that I knew a word like that, did you?" That's all 'cos the word he used wasn't the same word as Mummy and Daddy use; it was a word that only boys use when they're in a naughty mood. At least I think that's right. I think maybe all boys use that word when they're teenagers and when they stop using the proper word that's in my biology dictionary, and they want to talk that way to prove that they have girlfriends. Or something like that.

I don't want to think about these things any more 'cos something feels wrong about it all. So I'm going to stop. I'm going to make myself stop by thinking about how Mummy would say, "Would you stop doing that *right now?!*" She'd say it in a sort of rhythm, with each word sort of hitting the quietness that you thought was good before because you were playing happily and you didn't know you were doing something wrong, until she came out and said so, and then you'd hear the rhythm and you'd know straight away that it was wrong, and then you'd stop. So that's the way I'm going to make myself stop thinking about what I don't want to think. I'm going to say, "Rose! Would you stop thinking about that *right now!*" And when I imitate Mummy like that, and when I can get the rhythm of her words exactly the same as Mummy, I feel a bit giggly and that's funny.

It's very good to be feeling giggly instead of sad, and it reminds me of how many people say that I'm a very happy girl, and they say I've got a lovely smile, and hasn't Rose got lovely big dimples! And they say it in an admiring voice, and I really like that, very much.

… which reminds me that coming out on this whole treat is very, very special and I mustn't – mustn't! – let anything make me forget that. And I can't wait to get back and see everyone 'cos they'll all know that I've been special enough to have had a huge treat and that will be so nice.

5

Film Shows

I can't work out how on earth I've managed to get myself into such a mess, but I'm in one now and I don't know what to do because something Dreadful might happen unless I can think of a way of stopping it, and I don't think I can and I don't know what to do, which is what's so terrible.

When Uncle George comes round for tea every Sunday, sometimes he brings his films for a treat. He's got a cine camera and he takes films that lots of people admire when he shows them like at Sunday school, or at a thing in church called the Men's Fellowship Group. Once he filmed our family when he took all of us out in his car, so we would have something to remember the outing by together.

Anyway we're very lucky in our family 'cos we don't have to wait until Uncle George sets up all his equipment at church to show his films to everyone. He knows us well enough for him to bring his equipment to our house, to let us see his films here, for a treat, and usually it *is* a treat. At least it always has been every time until the thing that happened when I went out with him on my own, which is what's gone wrong and what's worrying me. Until this one thing happened, I always got very excited every time we had a film show; and all five of us children get excited, and sometimes Mummy and Daddy invite other friends from church to come and see the films in our house 'cos it's a special occasion. And we children are allowed to stay up a little bit late after our bedtime: at least, if Mummy hasn't noticed that "Oh, time has flown by!" as she says, "because that film just transported us all to…" and she says the name of the place that Uncle George's film was of.

Sometimes she tests us children with questions about where the film was of, because she says we must expand our geography, but mine's very bad and usually Oliver and Philip answer most of the questions 'cos they're the oldest. And once Roger cheated and I saw, 'cos I saw him reading the box that Uncle George had taken his film out of, and it must've said all the places that the film was of, only Roger didn't say anything until the film was showing and then he said, out of the darkness, "Oh, isn't that…?" (I can't remember where the place was.) Mummy and Daddy and Uncle George and another church lady (I think it was Miss Marshall, who teaches me the piano and takes the school choir), were all very impressed and Mummy gave a proud kind of gasp while she said, taking her breath in, "Huuuuhhhh" (taking her breath *in*, not letting it out), "What a good boy! What a *good* boy! Where did you learn that?"

Roger didn't say he'd read it on the box. But he just enjoyed all the admiring things that everyone said, and I felt my burning feeling and I know I'm not very kind sometimes and I had to say sorry to God again that night. But I didn't think it was fair of Roger and I wanted to say what had really happened, but I knew that Roger would just argue and say he hadn't read the box. and he's so used to telling lies that you can never win over him, and I know that 'cos I've tried and now I know there's no point.

Anyway, what happens when Uncle George gives us a film show is that we always have to pull the curtains to make the drawing room as dark as possible. That always gives me a bit of a funny feeling if we've only just had tea and the sun's still shining 'cos it's summer, but you can only see the film if the curtains are closed and that's just how it is and it's easier in winter 'cos it's dark. Then Uncle George does a lot of fiddling with his machine while he's threading the film from one wheel at the front through to the other one at the back, going round special little channels, a bit like a sewing machine, and he has to make sure he only touches the white bit of film and we're not allowed to put our grubby paws anywhere near the table in case we put marks on the brown bit of film, which is where the picture is and we would spoil it.

When everything on the machine is all lined up, Uncle George switches on his projector, which makes a quite loud whirring noise, and before we switch the lights out he has to adjust the feet so the picture lands on the screen properly. And I like being the one that's allowed to switch off the lights, although usually Roger gets to do it because of being older than me but I think I do the timing better. You have to wait until the film has just exactly started and then – before you get caught racing in front of the screen – you rush to the place on the floor where you're going to sit, which I hope will be near the fire 'cos I like leaning back on the chair where Daddy's sitting and being beside the fire as well.

On a Sunday when Uncle George is going to show his films he needs to make two journeys from his car: one to carry in his big long tube thing that he opens out to make a white screen, and that's got a very particular smell of plastic and I think it smells very clean. Then he goes back and gets his projector that he places on a particular table that Daddy always gets out specially, and then Daddy finds a book that's exactly the correct thickness for Uncle George to balance his projector on so the picture lands on the screen.

Everyone says what a good filmer Uncle George is, which is probably true except I sometimes feel a bit sick when he shows his films 'cos the picture flickers a lot and it wobbles, and you get lots of white dots sometimes and then it's hard to see what the picture is of but you mustn't say that or you'd hurt Uncle George's feelings. He always brings a film after he's been on a holiday and he goes on really expensive holidays. Last year he went to Egypt and he called his film "The Pyramids", which Mummy said we must all remember. The Pyramids are one of the Wonders of the World that are very, very old.

Mummy nearly always tests us on things like where places are, or what date things happened. When we go in a train, whenever the train stops at a station Mummy looks up and asks, "Where's this, then?" If you've read the name of the station, you can answer first, and I've noticed that if I look out of the window when the train's slowing down and before it gets to the station, there's quite often a signal box outside the station, before you get there, and if I read *that* sign then I can be first to say where we are. My brothers haven't noticed that, and I'm not going to tell them 'cos it's my secret. I like it when I can say where we are first, 'cos that means that Mummy won't pick on me for the next question, which might be something that I don't know the answer to.

There's only this one thing that spoils the film shows for me nowadays, and it has completely stopped me from being able to enjoy him showing them. I don't like having this thing and it's a very big pity 'cos everyone else thinks the films are such a treat and they're all happy. When visitors come they always say on their way out of our house how relaxing an evening it was. I'd like them to be relaxing evenings for me as well, and I do know that seeing the films is such a very good treat and I always like being allowed to stay up a little bit late. I would enjoy it all just as much if only I didn't get frightened about this one thing that I don't know if something's going to happen about. But the trouble is that I'm the only one who knows about this, so I can't ask anyone else what might happen 'cos that would mean I have to tell them things they mustn't know about.

The trouble is that they'd think it was all my fault, which it probably was mostly although not completely I don't think. But anyway I can't ask anyone 'cos nobody else knows anything about it, except Uncle George of course but I don't want to ask him what's going to happen in case he's forgotten, which I hope he has, and I don't want to make him remember.

So what happens is that every time Uncle George asks Mummy and Daddy if they'd like him to bring his films, I have to watch very, very carefully 'cos I want to try to find out which film he's going to bring. Usually Daddy will answer first and he'll say, "Oh, George, that would be a great Event!" because Daddy's very good at making Events from things, and he makes things feel very special. I remember when Daddy even made an Event out of just stirring his tea cup 'cos I'd brought him a cup of tea in bed after he'd had an operation. I'd accidentally forgotten to put any teaspoons on the tray so when Daddy had put his sugar-lumps into the cup he'd sort of pointed to the cup and made a circling movement with his finger and he was wrinkling his nose until I realized what he was miming and I exclaimed, "Oh, no! Daddy, I'm so sorry! I forgot to bring you a teaspoon to stir your sugar!" It seemed a long way to go all the way back downstairs but Daddy said, "Wait a moment, I'm sure we can find a teaspoon somewhere…" and he was reaching down over the side of the bed, and moving pieces of paper and he was saying in a very happy voice, "Somehow…" and I was just about to set off downstairs to get a teaspoon for him when all of a sudden Daddy's face lit up and he said, "It's all right, dear!" He pulled off his spectacles and he held one end of the plastic arm that goes behind his ear, and he put that in his teacup and he started stirring with that. He looked at me with a very big grin and he said, "I've got a teaspoon, haven't I, dear? What's wrong with this?" He looked so mischievous, and he didn't actually say, "Mummy's not here", but I think he might have been thinking that. Certainly I was thinking that, but then I laughed 'cos Daddy was laughing and he said, "Who needs teaspoons from downstairs when I've got my own teaspoon right here?"

I like when Daddy makes fun Events, especially when it could have been a problem, and I think if Mummy had been there it would have been a problem and I'd have had to go downstairs to fetch a proper teaspoon.

But I don't think there's anything that Daddy could do for my problem about the films, and I'm definitely not going to say anything to him in case it makes me stop being his Darling Daughter, which would be absolutely terrible. Anyway I can't say anything to anyone about it 'cos it's so bad. I don't know how I got into such a bad situation and I don't usually and I wish I hadn't – I really wish that, and I wish there was something I could do.

The problem is that Uncle George has got some film of me, and if anybody saw it they wouldn't understand at all what had happened 'cos they'd think something else had. 'Cos it looks as if something different happened from what *did* happen.

And if Mummy saw any of it, she would be so cross that it would make her give me the worst punishment she's ever thought of. And the worst bit is that I know I deserve for her to be cross because of what the film looks like, 'cos the trouble is that it makes me look as if I was being naughty, which I didn't know I was being when I was doing it. I didn't even think about anything to do with naughtiness.

What happened was, it was just a beautiful day on one of our outings and for an extra-special treat we went to the seaside and Uncle George let me go paddling. But then I was skipping so much that I kept getting my clothes all splashed and Uncle George asked me if Mummy might be cross if they got wet from the sea or – worse – grubby from the sand. And suddenly I realized he was right so I got a bit frightened.

Then Uncle George had a brainwave and he said I could splash properly if I took my clothes off, which all of us children always do when we're in our garden at home when it's a very hot

GOODBYE PINK ROOM

day and we paddle in and out of the washing-up bowl, pretending it's a paddling pool. So I did that and I was very skippy and sing-y and I sang with Uncle George a bit like how I sing with Daddy, only Uncle George didn't sing too; he just smiled. He was very nice 'cos he let me have such fun, and he enjoyed it too.

I could tell that Uncle George was happy and that he knew that I was happy, because he suggested that I could do some dancing because he knows I go to dancing classes. So I *did* do some dancing and splashing and paddling on the beach, and it was so much fun we were both laughing. Uncle George asked if I was good enough to know some of the special dancing positions that you have to learn, and when I said "Yes", Uncle George said he'd like to see and he said I was very good at it, which was very nice of him. Not many people watch me dancing and I thought it was very kind of Uncle George to be so interested in me; just me. He truly must mean that I am a special little girl, just like he said the very first time when I went to tea at his house on my own.

Anyway, I told him I could do handstands and cartwheels as well, and he didn't believe me so I showed him and then he did believe me. He said I was so good at them that he would film me. While he was filming I felt very happy and maybe I started being a little bit silly but I thought it was just fun. I did things like I made mischief faces, and next I put my head down and peeped out at Uncle George from between my knees and I was laughing and Uncle George was filming. Maybe I got a bit like a show-off and I must have done, and I know that's bad because Daddy says it isn't nice to be "showy-offy" (he makes up fun words sometimes, so that he doesn't sound too serious when he's telling us off). But I didn't realize I was being showy-offy – I just thought I was playing – and I enjoyed it so much.

And then, on a completely different day, I suddenly saw that it had been terrible and I hadn't known. What happened was that we went back to Uncle George's house after one outing in his car and he asked me if I'd like to see the film, the one of the seaside. And I said very eagerly, "Ooh, yes please!" So he showed it to me.

And that was when I got most terribly scared. I saw the pictures completely in a way that I'd never thought of before, and that's what I've been frightened about ever since 'cos…

… I feel so ashamed about this…

… You see, it doesn't look like a film of me dancing or being happy. At least, some of it does. But the rest of it is a rude film. All you can see is my bottom, with my head poking out, and I look as if I'm being terribly, terribly naughty and rude.

When I saw it – when Uncle George showed it to me – I suddenly stopped being proud of my dancing and instead I felt very shocked. It was exactly like the kind of shocked I felt when he said that rude word when we went on our very first outing. When the film ended Uncle George said the worst thing, and this is what I keep thinking about and I have done ever since; it still keeps coming into my dreams and everything. What he said was, "I wonder what Mummy and Daddy would say if they saw what Rose had done at the seaside?"

I must have taken a big breath, like a gasp that might have showed him that I was scared, and Uncle George asked, "Is something wrong, Rose?" But I couldn't answer. I felt so sick I didn't know what to do.

I looked at him and saw that his eyes were shining with a sort of fierceness that I hadn't ever seen before.

I think if he ever shows that bit of film, it might all be so bad that I might die.

Uncle George didn't say anything else, or if he did I didn't hear him 'cos I just kept thinking about how terrible it would be if he showed it. I didn't want Daddy ever, ever to see that film 'cos it would spoil everything completely. Daddy would be so disappointed in me, 'cos I don't only look "showy-offy". It's all much worse than that. And of course Mummy must never, ever see it because of how cross she would be.

I wondered what punishment I would get, and I couldn't stop thinking about it 'cos I knew that none of the punishments I could think of were bad enough for this rude, rude film of me being so terribly naughty.

So that's the whole reason why I get frightened every time we have a film show. Every time we have one nowadays I start to feel sick, just in case Uncle George shows this film. He might think that it would be a surprise, and I don't know if he realizes that if he showed it, it would make Mummy and Daddy think that I'm the most terribly naughty and rude little girl. They mustn't ever see it but I don't know if Uncle George realizes that.

Some people get themselves into a mess, and Daddy calls it getting into a Pickle – but the thing about them is that they're used to being in a mess and they know how to get round it. Some people tell untruths or half-truths, and they say that it's all right to tell a half-truth as long as you say one bit that is totally honest truth, but you must remember exactly what you haven't said. But I'm not used to doing that, and I've never practised, and I'm frightened that I might get it wrong. I might forget and then get in a tangle, which is what I'm in already. And anyway I don't want to become a Baddie, and the only reason why I'm thinking about how they manage is that I'm wondering if there's a way I can say part of the truth and not say another part, and would that help me now?

What I really want is to be ready with what to say if Mummy and Daddy find out this thing about me that I know is really terrible, but actually I think that there's nothing that I'll be able to say. 'Cos if I try to explain, Mummy's bound to keep asking me questions until she's got "the truth, the whole truth, and nothing but the truth". And what she doesn't understand is that I can't say everything 'cos it's not like what she'll think.

The thing is, people say that "cameras don't lie". That means that everyone'll think it's the real story, and there won't be any way anyone'll listen to it being different from that.

But what Mummy and Daddy wouldn't understand is that I think that that bit of film is like a sort of lie. I would need someone to explain that to them, and there's nobody who could. And what's become much worse is that I get so scared whenever I see Uncle George holding it ready to show it to them if ever I'm not good enough at doing what he tells me to do. He's said that to me. So if he shows the film at home, I couldn't explain everything, 'cos I don't think I could speak at all. Nothing I say will be big enough to work.

So all I can hope is that Uncle George will keep what I've done as a complete secret, and that he'll never ever tell them or show them. Which is why I try to be very, very good and always do what he says. Always, even if I don't like it very much.

Everything's gone all wrong for it to feel like this. I really didn't mean to be bad.

I am very, very sad.

6

The Christmas Present

It's Christmas Eve, which is one of the most exciting days in the world. I love Christmas Eve because the same exciting things always happen and we do things slightly differently from my friends: that's 'cos we do it the German way because Granny and Granddad used to live in Germany. I don't know very much about Granddad because he died when Mummy was very young and I've hardly ever heard Granny talk about him even though she must be sad about it sometimes, but she says that we thank God for His goodness and we don't dwell on the past. Her face goes a bit set, with her lips pursed in the same shape as if she was going to give a kiss, except I know that she's not going to give a kiss at all 'cos I can tell that she's nearly a bit angry. Her eyes look a bit cold and I don't like that. So that's how I know we're really not allowed to talk about the past and I mustn't ask any more questions. We have to forget about the past and look to the future.

Anyway, one of the things that's very special about my Granny from Germany is how she's taught us a lovely way to celebrate Christmas. That's why in our family we do lots of special things on Christmas Eve, which is today, and that's why I'm very excited. And I'm excited 'cos we've had our lovely special tea with lots of things that I've been baking. I've been so busy this morning that Mummy said I'm the best little helper and she looked very happy when I showed her the shortbread, and when I showed her the yule log that I'd made she gave a big sort of gasp she was so surprised, and I could tell that she was very, very pleased with me. I was very pleased with how it looked as well, especially when I'd decided how I could make a pattern on the chocolate icing to make it look like a log. I'd taken a fork and I'd made a pattern that was like the pattern of the bark on a tree. We've never had a yule log before and this year was the first time I'd made one, but I'd found the recipe in Granny's cookbook and I'd planned how to do it in school before our term finished last week.

When I passed the yule log round for Uncle George and Uncle Eric and Aunt Evelyn, they all admired it very much, and I felt very happy inside. On Christmas Eve we have extra treats and not just the normal Sunday sandwiches and fairy cakes. Sometimes we have crisps but this year we've got Twiglets, and when I passed them round I said I think we've got a theme of trees this year because we'd got a log and we've got little twigs. Everybody laughed because they hadn't noticed that the logs and the twigs both belong to trees. Of course we've got the Christmas tree as well, and logs on the fire, so that's why this Christmas we've got such a theme of trees.

We don't just have special food on Christmas Eve; we also do exciting things, such as singing carols all together round the piano which Mummy or Daddy plays. Aunt Evelyn's voice is a bit wobbly and everyone says she has a lovely voice except I think she sings a bit too loudly really. Her wobble is louder than anyone else so if you have a sweet voice, like Julian used to have, you get drowned out. But I mustn't say that sort of thing to anyone of course; I'm only thinking it, which makes it a secret.

In between carols we take it in turns to play or to sing a solo, and we're allowed to choose what we'll do. This year I'm going to sing a duet with Oliver. We've been practising our carol lots and I like it 'cos it means I've been with Oliver on his own. He doesn't usually tease me when he's on his own with me; he only does when he's with all the others.

Before we start singing, which is soon from now – it's as soon as we finish opening our presents – we'll light the candles on the Christmas tree. Everyone else has electric lights, which is just a foolish imitation of the real thing. I once heard Mummy say that.

I like it when Mummy's pleased with me and she's been very pleased with me all day today. I think she's happy 'cos she likes having other people to our house – she calls it entertaining – although she doesn't like doing baking but I like doing that. So when I bake shortbread and cakes and decorate the plates to look very dainty she gets very pleased with me and I like that.

We've very nearly finished opening our presents and Roger and I are sharing the job of handing the parcels around. I'm the one that reaches underneath the tree to choose a parcel and then Roger reads the name on it so he can carry it to the correct person. That's why I'm near the tree all the time, and I'm not so much in the circle of everyone, 'cos they know I'm either crawling underneath the tree to collect the parcels that are almost out of reach, or else I'm sitting on the floor beside it waiting for it to be time to get the next one.

There's only one more parcel for me to open and that's from Aunty Vi and Uncle Andrew, who live a long way away. I like the presents they give 'cos Aunty Vi always seems to know what I will like. I don't like the presents that Aunt Dorothy gives, although I'd never say that 'cos I know it's ungrateful. It's just that she gives things that we can never use and they're not pretty.

While Roger's giving out the other presents I'm wondering what this present is, because it feels soft and it's small enough to fit in my hand. It might be some new socks that are very white. I like having new white socks and I like choosing the pattern but I know that if Aunty Vi's chosen them, they'll be nice dainty ones. Or maybe she's given me some hankies with pretty embroidery on them, and if they are, Aunty Vi will have chosen something like an embroidered rose on them so that they match my name.

Mummy says that she and Daddy think that I'm the best rose in the world. At least, she says that when she's not rushing.

Last year Aunty Vi gave me a manicure set in a lovely pouch that was made in the shape of a heart. Mummy said I didn't need something that was only to do with vanity and she seemed a bit irritated but I liked it and I felt grown up having a manicure set 'cos that's what grown-up ladies have.

Roger's taken the last present to the last person, so that means I'm allowed to open my last present, too. I'm dying to see what Aunty Vi's chosen for me this year.

I've undone the sellotape and I've pulled apart the tissue paper and I'm looking at the white material and I don't recognize what this is. It's not hankies and it's not socks. I'm opening it out and there's elastic and there's lacy material which is pretty and…

… I've stopped opening this present out. I've put the wrapping back on and I pushed the little packet very quickly behind the pile of my other presents of the books and writing paper and soap and things. I really hope nobody sees me and I'm very glad I'm on the floor over here and I hope nobody notices me and especially I hope nobody asks to see what I've got. 'Cos I think that Aunty Vi has sent me a bra.

I don't want to get back up to sit back on my chair and I don't want anyone to see it, especially not Uncle George.

I don't need a bra, even though I've started at the Big School now and I'm called a Senior.

I think I may be blushing. My face feels very hot.

What can I do?

I was very excited before and I know I ought to stay very excited and I'm going to have to make myself look very happy in a minute 'cos we're all going to get up to sing together, but I don't know how to look the same.

What if Mummy asks me what I've got? In fact, Daddy's bound to ask me 'cos he's making a list of all the presents that we've all got, and he always does that and makes sure his list is completely perfect so that we all write our thank-you letters. So that means that he's going to notice in a minute and he's going to ask me what he should write for me under Uncle Andrew and Aunty Vi's name.

What shall I answer him?

I feel very, very shy. I'm frightened I might cry. That would be so terrible. Can I hide somewhere? What can I do?

I want to go upstairs to my pink bedroom and look at my teddy and maybe talk to him, although I know I'm not really talking to him 'cos he can't hear. But I don't want to be in here. 'Cos if I tell Daddy what I've been given, then everyone might hear, including Uncle George, and it might make him think I'm getting bosoms and then he might ask me again next time we go for a treat, and I don't want him to be reminded about that subject 'cos that would spoil the treat. And I want to keep going out with him 'cos he understands me so much, especially about Mummy.

Oh no. My heart is thumping. Mummy's asking me what I got from Aunt Vi.

My mouth has gone all dry.

I can't speak.

At least, maybe I can but I don't know what to say.

But I mustn't take a long time 'cos that'll let there be a silence and then it'll be worse 'cos everyone will be more ready to laugh.

Mummy's asking me to show it to her now.

What can I do?

Everyone's listening and they're all looking at me. If I show it to Mummy, then that will let everyone see. Including Uncle George.

If I'm not very, very careful I might cry, which I mustn't do, and I don't know how I'm going to stop myself.

Uncle George is looking at me too and I wish today weren't happening, and I never thought I'd ever say that about Christmas Eve.

. . . .

THE CHRISTMAS PRESENT 73

Mummy's telling me to "Come along, Rose!" Oh, help… help!

If I make a joke then everyone will laugh at my joke and then they might not laugh so much at me and at the fact that I don't need a bra.

I don't want them all to laugh at me. I don't want all my brothers to laugh. Just 'cos they don't have to be a girl, they laugh at anything to do with me being a girl. They laugh when I'm a cry-baby and they laugh when I'm a slow-coach on our bikes and they laugh at lots of things. I try to be like them, and at least I do manage to ride my bike almost as fast as boys go. But I don't completely want to be a boy 'cos I like being Daddy's Darling Daughter and only a girl can be that.

I've got to be quick 'cos everyone's waiting and I mustn't let them wait any longer.

I've taken a breath and I can hear myself talking. I'm putting on an accent so that I sound like Miss Brodie from *The Prime of Miss Jean Brodie*. Miss Brodie was a posh lady who sounded posh 'cos she was a teacher from the poshest area in Edinburgh. Sometimes in our family we have fun all together and especially Aunty Vi is very good at imitating Miss Brodie's posh Scottish accent. She makes us all laugh and giggle very much.

I'm trying very, very hard to do an imitation of Miss Brodie the same way that Aunty Vi does. Oh no, I've got to try very, very hard otherwise I might just burst into tears.

Rose! You've *got* to sound happy!

"This is a device," I hear my voice saying and I'm sounding as if I'm feeling strong and fun, even though inside myself I am crying. "It's a device to make mountains out of molehills."

I can see that I'm going to have to show everyone, so I pull the bra out of its tissue paper, properly, and just so everyone laughs at IT instead of at ME I'm swinging it round and round above my head. I'm laughing now and everyone's laughing, so that makes it a little bit easier for me so I don't need to cry. Look, I can laugh instead and that is forcing my tears to go away. Silly tears! They belong "down the drain", as Mummy would say.

My throat is feeling as if it's got a lump in it and I'm feeling so shy inside, even though I've been pretending that I'm not shy at all. But I'm packing up my presents now and when everyone stands up to sing, I'm going to take my pile of presents upstairs very quickly while everyone else is gathering round the piano. I'm going to do that just in case somebody else gets hold of my bra, like one of my brothers, especially Roger, who might take it and then tease me with it by dangling it in front of my nose.

The biggest reason that I want to run upstairs very quickly is that, when everyone was laughing and I was laughing and we were all supposed to be having a lovely time, I saw Uncle George's face. I didn't look at it for very long 'cos I knew I had to keep laughing otherwise I might get too embarrassed, but I saw it for long enough to see he had a funny look. It was funny-peculiar, not funny-ha-ha. I don't know what his look meant but his eyes had an extra sort of sparkle, and it wasn't very nice. He looked at… he looked to the place where I don't need a bra, and then he looked downwards as well, and I got a prickly sort of feeling inside myself when he did. But then he gave me a very big smile, and I didn't know what to do, so then I looked away from him.

I mustn't think about Uncle George's funny-peculiar look 'cos we have to count our blessings. Granny says that she counts her blessings when I ask her about difficult things. And she says that counting our blessings is what God wants, and it's bad to look at the difficulties in life 'cos they only make us be miserable. And she's never miserable about Granddad having died, so she must be right.

I wish I could make myself be more like Granny, 'cos I really don't want to cry but I can feel how nearly I am, and Granny must have a secret way of stopping herself, which must be why I've never seen her crying.

And anyway it's in the Bible to count your blessings so that means we really must. So as soon as I've been upstairs I'm going to manage to come back down by counting my blessings. It's a blessing that we're going to sing carols, which I really like doing, and then it's going to be a blessing afterwards that I'm going to be allowed to go to the midnight communion service in church. I'm old enough now, and this is the first year 'cos I started at Big School this year, in September.

And there's another blessing for me to count, which is that I'm at the best school and that's only possible by Uncle George paying for me, 'cos Mummy was so upset when I didn't get a scholarship like they wanted me to. She kept saying, "What shall we do?", because she and Daddy were "working their guts out" and they still didn't have enough money to pay for me, and I had to be at the best school because education is so important. That was when Uncle George asked to come and see Mummy and Daddy about a "serious matter", and he did. I had to stay in my room while they talked so all I know is that Mummy and Daddy both came upstairs when he'd gone. They were very solemn and they said that we are enormously indebted to Uncle George for his huge generosity, and he is such a kind man and I must never, never forget that.

That's why I'm now at that school and I like it very much.

And that's why Uncle George keeps taking me for treats, to help me to keep knowing how happy he is to support me at that school.

I still don't know why he gave me that funny-peculiar look and I wish he hadn't and I feel a bit frightened. But everyone's getting ready to sing now, so I must rush upstairs with my pile, and I'll give teddy a big kiss to say Happy Christmas. I'll come back down and I'll sing and then I'll do my duet with Oliver and then we'll

GOODBYE PINK ROOM

all go to church. So then everything will be back to being the very specially exciting time 'cos Christmas is like that, and I must count my blessings.

Passage of Time (1)

Several months
Several trips
Outwardly "normal"

7

It's Raining Today

I'm sitting in the front seat of the car and I'm watching drops of rain land on the window next to me. It's raining today, which is why Uncle George says we've got to stay in the car. I wanted to get out because… because…

I've waited quite a long time to say because of *what*, 'cos I don't want to be naughty, and saying why-because would be naughty, 'cos it has rude words. But also I do want to say it to myself 'cos that will help me to make sure that it isn't naughty. I think the *real* reason to say why-because isn't naughty, but the trouble is that most people wouldn't stay to listen to the real reason. They'd just say it *is* naughty.

I'm going to try again to say in words to myself why-because, although it's nicer just to watch the drops falling on this window. They land quite gently, and I want to think about "gently", which is a nice word and a nice thing.

"Gently".

I like thinking about "gently".

I'm ready now to start again to say why-because.

The reason I wanted to get out of the car is because…

… well, I know I'm not supposed to say this, but the reason I wanted to get out was because I don't like what he's doing and I didn't like how he was talking before he started doing things, but I know it's not polite to say if we don't like things. Mummy says I mustn't be selfish, it's bad to be selfish, and Daddy says I'm not a selfish girl. In fact, he once said to me that I'm one of the most thoughtful little girls he knows and I like when he talks like that 'cos he makes me feel very special. I like feeling special to Daddy and especially when he calls me "My Darling Daughter". He says it as if that's my name, which is why I think of the three words in capital letters. "And how's My Darling Daughter?" he says as soon as he sees me whenever he comes in from work – at least, when he's in a good mood he says that, and when he's not rushed or when he's not arguing with Mummy. When he says it he has a smile, a nice smile, so I think (inside myself) he's pleased he's found a way of putting his happiness into words. Anyway, so I want Daddy to stay pleased with me, and I never want to do something that might stop me from being his Darling Daughter, and that's why I don't want to be selfish.

And I don't want to be selfish 'cos Mummy says that selfishness is bad, too, only I think that she's a bit more strict than Daddy. But then Mummy quotes Granny, who was never selfish and everyone loved her, and then there's Granddad, who I think must have been very strict as well, even though I know I shouldn't really say that because I mustn't criticize him because he's dead and you're not allowed to say bad things about dead people. And anyway everyone loved him very, very much. But when I'm on my own, I think he must have been terribly strict because he taught Mummy lessons when she was only three and she had to learn everything and lots of poetry and lots of the Bible, all off by heart, and if she got anything wrong then Granddad sent her to her room with dry bread and water, and I think that's very strict when you're only three. But Not Being Selfish is something that everybody in all the family talks about, and they all say the same so I know it must be an important rule. So that's why I don't want to be selfish and that's why I mustn't tell Uncle George that I don't like being in the car.

Mummy says that one of the signs of being Selfish is when you start a sentence with, "I don't like…". I remember when I had a birthday party and I was allowed about six friends, which was a lot, and we all sat down for tea and the table looked lovely and it had an extra-pretty cloth to show it was a special party. Mummy had made lovely egg sandwiches and she'd put little bits of parsley on the side of the plate for decoration, which also showed it was a special party.

One girl called Beccy said, "I don't like egg!" and Mummy was very cross even though she didn't say so at first. Then Mummy put some crisps on the table, which was a very, *very* big treat 'cos we're never allowed crisps in our family 'cos they're for people who waste their money and we can't waste ours. Beccy asked what flavour they were and Mummy said "Plain", and Beccy said, "I don't like plain crisps!" I saw that Mummy was getting crosser and crosser because her lips stayed together in a way that I know means she's cross. My friend Ruth who was sitting next to me nudged me 'cos she knew that you're not allowed to say, "I don't like" in my house. But Beccy didn't know 'cos she hadn't been for tea before.

The worst thing of all happened when Mummy brought out some biscuits with raisins in, and Beccy asked what were the "bits" in the biscuit. Mummy didn't answer her properly but she looked at her with a very stern face for a long time and then she said, "Listen here, young lady…" I thought oops, and I felt as if I was going red. I could have giggled with Ruth except fortunately I didn't, but I only managed to stop myself because Ruth didn't giggle either. Then Mummy said to Beccy, "I think you had better decide whether you want to stay at this party, or should I take you home right now? Because if I hear those words 'I don't like' one more time" (and here Mummy put on a very, very high-pitched voice so she sounded very funny-peculiar), "let me tell you that you're going to regret ever coming here, and so am I."

Ruth and I very nearly got the giggles, but I was watching Mummy's face carefully and I knew that she was very angry so I would have got into Terrible Trouble if I had giggled, so instead I only thought about how serious it was to say "I don't like" and I mustn't say that.

I don't want to say to Uncle George that I don't like what he's doing, but the trouble is I don't like it, so that's why I'm watching the rain landing on the window 'cos that helps me to not think about him.

I want to be a good girl, a not-selfish girl, so I mustn't say anything naughty if I don't like things. I want to stay Daddy's Darling Daughter.

I'm concentrating quite hard on the drops and I'm thinking that if you watch very carefully how they land, they don't land very hard, which you expect them to do. In fact each drop sort of strokes the window when it lands. It's a gentle kind of stroking, but I mustn't let myself think about stroking now in case I think about what Uncle George is doing and I mustn't do that in case I cry. Only babies cry. Mummy says that whenever I cry after she's said there's no need to. Often when any of us children in our family cries, then the others of us will chant at them, "Cry-baby! Cry-baby!"

I don't want to be a cry-baby.

I did try to say to Uncle George very politely that I would like to get out of the car. Earlier, I mean. Before he started doing this. I didn't say I didn't want Uncle George to do anything; I didn't use the bad words "I don't want…". I tried to be very, very careful so that I wouldn't be impolite or nasty towards him, and I just said in a happy voice that I like being outside and I said maybe we could have a bit of fun outside, couldn't we, even though it was raining? I said I like running in the rain and getting the taste of the raindrops in my mouth. You can do that if you stand in the rain and tilt your head backwards and upwards and hold your mouth open wide – one time a raindrop will land on your tongue. And I laughed 'cos I wasn't sure whether it was maybe a bit rude

GOODBYE PINK ROOM

to hold your mouth open in the rain. Mummy says if you want to know if something's rude, then you ask yourself if the Queen would do it, and I don't think the Queen would stand in the rain with her mouth open waiting to taste the flavour of the rain. But even if she wouldn't do that, I like doing it and Uncle George told me that the reason for him taking me out in the car was so we could have FUN together, which is why I think it should have been all right for me to have suggested playing in the rain outside the car.

But the trouble is that when I said that, I made Uncle George put his arm round me and say we could have fun inside the car, and he said that he'd make sure it really *was* fun as long as I was a very good girl. I wanted to wriggle away but I knew I mustn't do that and I knew I mustn't say "I don't want…", because I knew I mustn't be like Beccy, so I didn't say it.

But inside myself I don't want this. I don't; I don't!

I wish I hadn't said to Uncle George that we could have a bit of fun outside, because that's what made him put his arm round me and I wish I didn't do things to make him put his arm round me. That shows that it must be all my fault, what's happening now, because I made it start. But the trouble is, I never know in time. It's only after he's put his arm round me that I realize that I've made him do that.

And I did worse than that, because I talked about opening mouths and about my tongue, and that made him talk about some of those things that I'm not going to think about now, but what I know and I wish I didn't know. When he told me about kissing and things, and I didn't understand properly, he said he'd have to show me what he meant so that I would understand. Otherwise I won't be able to grow up to be a real lady, and I want to do that.

I really, really wish I hadn't made all this happen but I'm going to try to stop thinking about it and think only about the raining.

I am looking at the raindrops, and I am thinking about them, but also I'm deciding that I mustn't think about what I wish 'cos that's selfish.

What I'll have to do instead is I must concentrate more on the raindrops and what I'm going to do is look at just one raindrop and think about that.

8

The Bough That Doesn't Break

I'm puzzled. I'm sitting up on my branch of a tree that I've climbed in the park opposite our house. I like the way that this is completely *my* branch. It's exactly the right shape for me to sit here. It's as if the branch has got cupped hands and I sit where they hold each other and I feel as if they almost hug me very safely.

The proper word for a branch is a bough, and a long time ago I learned the nursery rhyme about "When the bough breaks…". But *my* branch won't break 'cos the tree is so old that the bough's grown thick and strong, so my branch is better than the nursery rhyme. That's why I feel safe here.

I'm trying to work everything out in my head and I have been ever since I was in the car when I just managed to stop my brain from bursting. The problem is that I still feel very puzzled even though I've been thinking about everything quite a lot of times now. I don't like still being puzzled after I've tried so hard, 'cos that seems as if I must be stupid and I don't think I am stupid really. I hope I'm not. Anyway I want to try to finish working everything out this time, 'cos I'm tired of trying. Once I've got everything sorted all out, completely, forever, then I won't need to try any more, so I've chosen to do it here so I can concentrate properly on my own and not have to get interrupted.

I don't think anybody knows I'm here. I hope they don't know 'cos then they won't come and tell me that I must come in, or tell me that I must be getting cold or – if I say I don't want to come in – tell me that I *have* to come in to set the table. And then I really would have to go in.

I like the feeling inside myself when nobody knows where I am. I feel a bit like the King of the castle. (I ought to say Queen of the castle, because of being a girl!) I sit here and think and I sit knowing I'm on my own. I am almost certain that nobody would see me if they looked for me out of the window 'cos people usually look at the swings and the climbing frame, and they don't look up into the tree. Anyway I sit very still when I'm up here which means that I don't make the branches shake. This makes me be different from when my brothers or other children climb this tree 'cos anyone can see when they are climbing in it. They make the branches all sway about and the whole tree makes a shaking noise 'cos they have races to see who can be fastest to get up it. They're rough when they climb this tree, but I'm gentle. I'm not like them at the moment, and I'm not moving at all. I'm keeping very still and very quiet.

I keep still like this when he does things to me and tells me rude things that I don't like. One reason why I keep very *still* when he's doing the things is 'cos I think that God will notice that I'm not moving so He'll notice that it's not me doing anything, and I don't know how to stop it but maybe keeping very still might help. And one reason I keep very *quiet* when he's telling me things is 'cos sometimes at home when someone gets the blame for something and they say it's not their fault, I've heard Mummy say, "Well, you encouraged him!" It sounds as if that means it sort of IS their fault. At least I think that. A bit, anyway.

I don't want to "encourage" Uncle George, which is why I keep very, very quiet. I'm thinking in a whisper now, 'cos I don't want to think this in a loud voice, and what I think is that if I always keep very, very still AND very, very quiet, then maybe I'll manage not to "encourage" him and maybe it'll stop sooner and maybe God will notice that I don't want this to happen.

I hope that bit very much. Very, very much.

I wish Jesus would make everything stop happening. Or maybe He could just come and ask Uncle George nicely if he would stop doing it.

Why doesn't Jesus do that?

I think that if Jesus asked Uncle George not to do it, he would probably do what Jesus said because he goes to church every week, so I'm sure he'd listen to Jesus.

Maybe Jesus hasn't asked him not to do it to me, which would mean that him doing everything has got to be all right. Uncle George does say it's all right, but it's just that I don't really feel as if it's nice. But he says it's definitely all right. He says that what he teaches me is all an important part of me growing up to be a big girl. I want to grow up to be a big girl 'cos I don't like if my brothers chant at me anything about me being a baby, so maybe some bits of becoming big are very good but they just don't feel very nice.

But the main thing of what I'm puzzled about is something else.

The trouble is, I've been sitting up here for quite a while now and I still haven't got to the bit I was supposed to be working out, but I don't think I can work it out any more 'cos I can't remember it any more. That's very annoying 'cos I wanted to finish getting everything all worked out today. This keeps on happening lots of the time, and it happens with the new things that happened last Saturday that I have to work out and it happens with things that I have to work out for school. I try to work everything out and, if I can't, I promise myself I'll do it later, and then by the time later arrives and I find a good place all on my own to think properly and sort everything out, I start thinking about other things and then I can't remember what I needed to work out in the first place. I wish I could forget about everything forever, but I can't because…

. . . .

… because…

… because the reason I can't is…

… the reason is that…

I'm being silent now so I'm not even going to whisper.

…

And I'm going to stay like this for a long time.

…

Oh dear. My sleeve's just got a little circle dot of darkness on it, and I just noticed the wetness arrive there. That's because a tear has fallen onto my sleeve, which shows that I'm sort of crying, but only very softly and very gently, and it's only by mistake. Nobody will know 'cos nobody can see me, and nobody's come to shout for me to come inside which is nice, mostly, but a little bit of it's not nice 'cos I'd quite like it actually if someone could be missing me.

I am a bit cold but I sort of want to be, and I think I understand something about why I do.

Sometimes I want to be cold 'cos when I'm very, very cold I can't think at all; I just become like ice and snow and I imagine a picture of winter whiteness that's got nothing in it and everything has been made all white, all the same, and then I don't remember anything nasty at all. It's all white which is much better than white with black which is what I feel like on lots of the Saturdays if Uncle George has lifted up any of my clothes. Even afterwards I always still feel as if the horrible things I've had to do for him have got stuck on me, a bit like black bits that get blobbed onto a pretty white dress.

I haven't got a white dress but I have got a pink one and I like being a girl with a pink bedroom and other people like it too, especially Granny and Daddy who say so.

And sometimes… sometimes I want to be cold 'cos if I'm cold that helps me to remember what happened when I was cold for the reason that I don't like, which is that I didn't have enough clothes on because... because... because of everything. And although what I want most is to NOT think about that, I also DO want to think about it 'cos otherwise if I forget completely then I'll forget why I sometimes suddenly feel as if my head will burst.

Sometimes I don't know which is better: to remember or to forget. Usually I think it's better to forget and to make everything white, completely snow white, so that everything's all become a nothing. But when I do that then I get a very big rush of feeling that I've GOT to remember that I am forgetting, otherwise I'd have been silly 'cos I'd have been imagining everything.

But I wasn't imagining everything. I'm sure I wasn't, because...

... except, if I was imagining things, then everything would all be all right 'cos it would mean that everything didn't happen and I didn't see any rude things, or feel funny, or see something happen to Uncle George that I thought was very frightening indeed and very horrible.

I especially don't want to think about the horrible thing so I'm not going to. Instead I can concentrate on being cold.

Except sometimes I sort of don't want to be cold, 'cos when I get as cold as I've got right now, I begin to feel a bit sore as well as cold. That's when my fingers hurt, as if the cold has tried to bite me, and my toes hurt too, and I don't feel like moving AT ALL.

Now that I've begun to think of not moving I'm becoming even more mixed up. Oh, I'm too muddled now. I've got lost in my brain. I don't know if I want to be cold or not! 'Cos although I don't like the nasty feelings and the hurty feelings, I also think at the same time that all this is making me keep very, very still *indeed*, which is how much still I want myself to keep when Uncle George is doing things to me. So now I'm beginning to wonder whether this is actually good practice for being with him so I can keep still better. And maybe if I learn how to keep the best still, God will be more likely to notice me and He'll realize a bit more that it's not me doing it and that might make Jesus come and ask Uncle George to stop.

Why, oh why *doesn't* Jesus do that?

I don't know any more whether to keep keeping the very best still 'cos I'm so cold, or whether to get down from where I am, and creep back into the house and warm up (I could slide under my silky slidey quilt in my pink bedroom) 'cos I really, really don't like being as cold as I am now, which is getting even colder. I can feel all of my legs and arms feeling gnawed-at and by now I feel as if my head is absolutely and completely bursting.

I HATE THIS

I think I'm going to get down in a minute – in just a minute I will, but not quite yet 'cos I'm not completely ready yet – but I think I'll have to, 'cos I don't like my fingers and my toes biting me as they are doing.

I feel sad. I want to get down and I don't want to and I don't know what to do.

The funny thing is that the person who could help me best, I think, is Uncle George. One of the nice things about Uncle George is that he always remembers to ask me about what makes me unhappy, and then he helps me 'cos he has good answers because he's always understanding – every Saturday. He understands about how I get frightened when Mummy is strict; and sometimes he puts his arm round me and when he does only that one thing and doesn't do anything else, I like it 'cos he gives me a very warm hug. I would like a warm hug now because of being so cold and sad. And when I talk to Uncle George about what I don't like about my brothers or school or even Mummy or Daddy, he always looks so understanding and I know why everyone at church thinks he's so nice. Then I think I must be a very bad person because of the times when I've thought that he's not so nice. Or I've thought, "I don't like this," which makes me rude and naughty like Beccy.

I know it's naughty to say "I don't like…". I mustn't do it. It's cheeky, which is why it's not allowed.

If I mustn't say that, then it must be that Uncle George is nice, the way other people say he is. So I'm just going to forget all about the bits that I don't like and I'm only going to think about having a nice hug. He can do nice hugs. He does do them, every time he takes me out in his car. At least, at the beginning they're nice hugs and I always hope that he'll keep giving me those nice ones.

So I'm going to look forward to the next time I see Uncle George, and I'm going to think about the *good* bits about him. Which is what the Bible says to do: it says, "If there is anything good" (and it says a long list of good things), "think about these things."[1] So I'm going to think whatever is good about Uncle George and look forward to my next warm hug and then everything will be all right forever.

I'm going to say a prayer before I get down.

"Dear Jesus. Thank You for this tree being in the park and thank You for it having a bough that doesn't break. Thank You for my place in it where I get a sort of hug, even if it's only a tree and I'd prefer to have a person doing it. Thank You for helping me to feel better up here. Please bless Mummy and Daddy and Oliver and Philip and Julian and Roger and Uncle George and help me to love them better all the time and not think bad things about any of them. Please help me to get warmer when I've climbed down. Oh, and I'm sorry I thought bad things about my brothers too and please help me to love them more. Ahhh – arrrr – … MEN!"

(I like having fun singing the notes of "A-men" like just then, which I do when I'm very happy 'cos I've prayed, and now that I've prayed and I'm happy I can tell myself that everything is really, really going to be all right starting from… NOW!)

Jump!

---

1 Philippians 4:8 NLV.

9

Music Lesson

I'm standing next to Miss Marshall who's sitting on the piano stool, showing me how to play my piano piece. She can't see my face 'cos she's too busy showing me how I ought to hold my hands up from the keys.

I'm glad Miss Marshall can't see my face 'cos if she could, she might see that I'm feeling quite sad, although I'm not quite sure why.

I didn't learn my pieces this week, which I do normally, and I know I should have done. And I'm not sure why I didn't practise properly except I haven't felt sing-y this week and I don't feel sing-y now.

I like when I feel sing-y. I don't always need music to feel sing-y 'cos sometimes feeling sing-y is just like when I want to skip home from school. But with music, I feel sing-y sometimes with Mummy and sometimes with Daddy. I love when Mummy plays tunes on the piano, 'cos when she plays it she always giggles at the same time, and that makes me happy because of how I can giggle with her. But usually she doesn't have time. When she is going to play, you can tell 'cos she sort of jumps up from her chair and almost skips towards it, as if the piano helps her to get into a silly sort of mood or something, and she'll start her giggling before she's even sat down properly on the piano stool and suddenly she'll begin "Here comes the bride". Then when she gets to the end of that we laugh together, and if Mummy's got time she thinks of another tune that she can play. And then she plays a piece that sounds very difficult, and she never has any music 'cos she learned it all off by heart when she was a child. She tilts her head a little bit to one side, as if there's something far away that she can hear but I don't know what it is, and she never looks at her hands at all. I think she's very clever at doing that, and she looks quite beautiful, and I am puzzled about why she says she's not. Most times when I suggest that she might play the piano, she says, "Och, I'm no use at that any more! No! No use!" Except that's the moment when, sometimes – not always – she'll jump up and she *will* play, and I think that's a good thing and it makes us both feel sing-y.

I wish I could make myself feel sing-y today.

Sometimes Daddy and I sing together. I sing the songs from my Sunday school and hymns from our church, or one time what I sang was the music from a proper concert. That was when our whole family had had a huge treat one Christmas, and we went to hear a proper orchestra. I wore my very best dress with a white lace collar and I had socks that were properly white 'cos I'd got them new for Christmas so they hadn't gone grey, and I put my hat on as well with its velvet ribbon so I know I looked very nice and grown up.

That outing was all 'cos Uncle George goes to big concerts like this quite a lot, and he had bought extra tickets to take Mummy and Daddy and all of us children. I used not to be allowed to come 'cos they thought I was too young so they said I wouldn't be able to sit still for a whole concert, but Uncle George said that he'd included me because I was old enough because I'm growing up. When he said that, Mummy and Daddy both looked very pleased, as if it was a compliment to them, and they both looked over to me to make sure that I would say "Thank you very much" to Uncle George, which I did.

While they were looking at me Uncle George was also looking at me – which they didn't actually notice – and he gave me a special sort of look, which was a very big smile and a sort of wink. And I know that is the expression he makes when he is being very kind although sometimes I don't like it, a bit, which is very bad of me and very ungrateful and I don't want to be those things so I'm trying not to think the wrong thing.

Everybody knows that Uncle George is a very kind man and they all say so and he keeps doing kind things like taking our whole family to the concert. And I think that's one reason why I'm not feeling very sing-y today, 'cos I know Uncle George is kind and yet I wasn't happy after his special treat last Saturday when he took me out again. I don't quite understand why, especially 'cos I've been trying to make myself be. I'm frightened that this might be a sign that I'm growing up to be an ungrateful person. Mummy and Daddy have taught me that what makes a person ungrateful is that they don't know what's good for them and I think they must be right.

So I mustn't let myself get ungrateful for Uncle George's kindness.

I mustn't tell Mummy or Daddy or let them find out that sometimes I don't feel grateful at all. I do try very hard to make them see me saying "Thank you".

The trouble is, I accidentally find myself thinking about Uncle George's treats at times when I shouldn't, like now. It's as if my mind has got a slide inside it, and my thoughts keep sliding down from what I'm supposed to be concentrating on – like Miss Marshall and her piano playing and how I ought to hold my hands – but my thoughts slide down from there and they land at the bottom of the chute where I find myself thinking about what happens with Uncle George. Which I don't really want to do, 'cos I like music and I want to learn so that I can play out loud some of the songs that live inside me.

Miss Marshall has a smell that I don't like very much. I don't like when I have to stand next to her when she's seated at the piano 'cos it means that my nose is much closer to her mouth, so when she speaks her breath falls straight onto my face and I can't get away. I don't like that and sometimes I find that I haven't listened to her properly 'cos I've been trying to block my nose and not sniff up while she's talking, and I've thought about that instead of thinking about what she's been teaching me. And then suddenly she'll say, "Rose!" very loudly, and that'll make me jump in a startled kind of way, and I'll look at her, and her face will look quite fierce and just a few times I've thought I don't like her very much really. I'm not supposed to think that, which is why I ask God to help me to try to love her the way He wants us to love everyone.

Miss Marshall is getting up now and I've got to play my piece holding my hands in the same way as she held her hands. I think it's worse when we change round and she stands next to me while I am seated on the stool, 'cos that means that my nose is very close to a part of Miss Marshall that is a rude place and I really don't like that smell. Mummy says that she thinks Miss Marshall might "have problems" and I'm not sure what she means but I once heard that, sometimes, some people wet themselves – but only a very tiny bit. I just wish she would move further away from my nose a little bit. Just one step would be better than her being this close.

The thing is, smelling Miss Marshall like I am now is making me remember the thing that I keep worrying about every time I think about it, which I try not to do but sometimes I just can't help it, like now.

The bit that worries me is that…

… I feel so ashamed…

… The thing is that, last Saturday when I went out with Uncle George, after we had had a picnic outside the car and we were on his tartan picnic rug, sort of sitting and sort of lying down, and…

· ·

… I just mustn't let myself think about this. It's just that Miss Marshall is standing so close to me that the smell is forcing me to remember the dreadful thing…

… This particular thing has never happened before last Saturday, and I'm very worried in case it might make me become the same as Miss Marshall and have a "problem".

I wouldn't think about it at all except for how Miss Marshall is standing here, and what's worrying me is in case I got a smell after… after…

… after he'd finished. And everything.

I must concentrate on what Miss Marshall is saying, except I'm finding it very hard because of what I'm worrying about.

Miss Marshall is one of Uncle George's friends. She doesn't talk about Uncle George to me but she does to Mummy and Daddy and anyway I see them together. They both go to our church and they both go to concerts and Miss Marshall was at the concert that I went to. She said she was glad that I'd gone to that concert and I ought to go to more. I don't think she knows that our family can't afford that sort of thing and we can only go when Uncle George gives us that treat as a sign of his kindness.

Miss Marshall has just startled me, and I jumped. She gave me a big fright 'cos I wasn't expecting her suddenly to shout. She told me that I wasn't holding my hands firmly enough when I began playing my piece. She didn't let me play very many notes before she interrupted and she said, "Higher, Rose. Higher." I didn't know what she meant and I wondered if she meant that she wanted me to play my piece an octave higher or something, until she said, "Hold those wrists higher!"

When I still didn't understand enough, 'cos I don't think I'd been listening to her properly earlier, she said, "Lift those wrists, and allow your fingers to fall from your knuckles. Relax your fingers – that's better now – but make sure you keep those hands of yours *above* the keyboard!" I did exactly what she said and I began to play again, only then her smell came even nearer to me 'cos she leaned forwards more and she started to use her hand to push the backs of my hands, almost as strongly as if she had been smacking them.

At first when she pushed like that, my hands sort of collapsed down onto the white notes and that made a terrible noise. She said very sternly, "Don't allow me to push your hands down! Keep them *up!*" She did the same pushing again, and she said again, "Come on, hold your hands more firmly; keep them up!" until I began to get cross at the horrible noise it made so I began to resist her whenever she hit my hands. I had to play my piece all the way through with her hitting me like that but without me letting my hands fall down onto the notes. At last she said, "Good!" but I didn't think that anything was good until she had stepped away from me a bit and then I could take a proper breath in without smelling her.

I wish I hadn't smelled that smell, 'cos that's what made me start getting worried about what I did, and the tartan rug, and I wish I could think only about my piano playing. But I can't concentrate properly at all now. I'm frightened 'cos if Miss Marshall asks me what's wrong, I won't be able to tell her.

What will I say?

What will happen if she asks me anything?

I won't be able to speak. I won't be able to explain anything. She might tell Mummy or Daddy or teachers at school or Uncle George or people at church or anyone at all.

I mustn't let that happen, 'cos then they would all start asking me questions and I don't know what I could say.

I'm looking down at my hands now and I'm listening, trying very hard to listen to Miss Marshall talking about resisting when someone pushes you. And that is sending my thoughts on to their slide, and they're sliding away from Miss Marshall and going back again down towards what happened with Uncle George.

"Resist when someone pushes…"

I wish there was someone I could ask about these things.

Miss Marshall just said that it's possible to keep going with the music and to have my hands set so well and so firmly that I can "resist anything that anyone else may do", and I can keep on playing and making beautiful music as long as I keep my hands set.

I want to make beautiful music. I want to do that in my piano playing and I want to do it always, altogether, in my life. Daddy would be very proud of me if I could make beautiful music in my life. And even more important than Daddy, I've learned that God loves us to make beautiful music with our lives, although I've never heard anyone say it like that; I just think it myself.

"You can do it, Rose. You've shown me right now that you can do it."

I've suddenly gone all shivery, ever since Miss Marshall started giving me this speech. She says it's just a question of being strong to resist properly.

Should I be able to "resist" Uncle George doing things? But how could I? You're not allowed to "resist" when grown-ups say you have to do things. Everything would just be very awkward and difficult, and he might tell Mummy that I hadn't been good.

I'm very frightened.

Miss Marshall says she's a little bit disappointed in me today, but that at least I've learned a bit more about maintaining my hand position, and she hopes I'll practise and learn it better. She says it would help me to remember how I resisted her pushing my hands.

The slide, the slide! My mind is going down it again, just hearing these words…

I wonder if people can make *every* part of them resist, no matter how other people press when you don't want them to?

If I learned to resist properly, would I be able to stop all the horribleness, just like I stopped the horrible noise on the piano when Miss Marshall wanted me to?

I think that I'm not good enough to do exactly what Miss Marshall says.

When I'm with Uncle George, I let him do the things he does, just like I had to let Miss Marshall do what she was doing to my hands. Except, it's different with Uncle George 'cos he doesn't touch my hands; he touches other places, which is why I can't tell anybody. It's too rude. And they would just tell me that I'm a very rude girl, if I did say the truth. Which is why I mustn't say anything.

Miss Marshall has gone over to her desk now and she's writing in my homework book and I'm watching her. I'm thinking about how it would be very nice if only I could ask some things about Saturday and about Uncle George, but actually I can't ask Miss Marshall. I don't think she would understand and it would be terrible if I tried and she didn't understand. For example, if I say to her now that I didn't like some things on Saturday, and if she asked me what I didn't like, and if I said I didn't like when Uncle George came so very near to me, she wouldn't understand 'cos she doesn't know that I don't like being close to *her* with her bad smell.

I wish I knew somebody who would just understand.

I know God understands, but the trouble with Him is that you can't see Him. And anyway He loves everybody, so that means that He loves Miss Marshall and it must mean that He doesn't mind her smell because He loves her so much He won't notice; and He loves Uncle George and it must be that He doesn't mind about… about… about everything.

So probably that means that I mustn't mind either.

So all this means that I mustn't say anything.

And anyway I feel polite inside myself and *I don't want to be a rude girl.*

It's just that I wish there could be someone that I could ask about some of Saturday's things that Uncle George did, and I keep looking everywhere to find someone. In Sunday school all the teachers – which includes Miss Marshall – they all say, "You can come to us if you have any problems – any problems at all, or any questions!" They don't seem to understand how it's not like that.

I wish I knew how to do what they say. They say, "We're here for you!"

It must be my fault if I don't go to them and ask them things that I don't understand.

I wish…

… Oh dear. I'm not sure what I wish.

I just feel a bit sad, and I wish I didn't feel sad, especially after a music lesson, which usually makes me feel very sing-y and usually I skip all the way home.

It's time to go home now, and I've got to leave Miss Marshall, and I won't have asked her anything. I'll walk home. Which isn't the best thing, 'cos Daddy calls me his very skippy, sing-y little girl, and I like being that. I don't want to be un-skippy.

I must try very hard to find my skip again.

10

What if He Tells?

One time, in the middle of us chatting together about everything, Uncle George said, "Well…" And there was a pause, and he was smiling (but it was a funny-peculiar sort of smile), and then he said, "I could certainly tell your mother some things about *you*…" And I suddenly got a very big shock. 'Cos the trouble is, I've always been so happy when he has listened to me, and he understands so well everything I say. I haven't ever even thought, before now, that he might store things up and actually tell Mummy some of the things I've said. In fact, I even remember that when I dropped the cake crumbs and laughed about Mummy, he promised not to tell. He *promised!*

It's the same with that bit of film of me, which he could show on any day when he comes and that's why I get worried every time we're going to have films. Everyone would think that I've been so naughty, 'cos that is what it would look like, and they would have sort of proof, and nobody would even start to believe me.

Anyway, what could I say?

I don't think I could say anything at all, even if someone asked me.

I feel completely ashamed of everything I've told Uncle George about Mummy, and I feel ashamed for using some of the words that he uses.

The only thing I can do to try to stop him (and I have tried to do this ever since he said that he could tell) is I can be extra careful that I do exactly what he says, so then he won't tell on me 'cos I'll have been good enough.

This is the first time that I've thought properly of how bad I've been. And yet I feel mixed up 'cos Uncle George is still being nice to me, and he did give me his extra-kind smile that always says, "Rose, I am here for your sake. You mustn't forget that."

But if he *did* ever tell Mummy and Daddy, they would be bound to believe him and not me because he's a person that everyone respects at the school where he teaches and in our church.

11

Latin Lesson

I've just looked across the classroom and noticed how Amanda places her hand when she's sitting. I must try to copy her 'cos I've just realized that maybe it's the angle she puts her hand that makes her look so grown up when she sits in class. Amanda's so grown up she doesn't wear socks any more. She has tights. And she has make-up. I would like to be more like Amanda, but I don't think Mummy likes her.

I will listen to Miss Flowers when she actually starts the textbook with us, but at the moment she's just talking to the people who didn't do their homework properly.

I like Latin. I like Miss Flowers. I like her 'cos whenever she talks to us in class, she doesn't call us "Girls", but "Ladies". She sweeps in very quickly, and often very quietly, and occasionally she comes in and stands at the front of the class before anyone's noticed (if we're all talking or, worse, if we're messing about). She simply stands there and waits, but she waits silently. The first time she did it was when she first started being our teacher. I was a bit frightened of her actually – just a bit anyway. I was afraid because not only (*"non solum… sed etiam…"* That's a phrase that Miss Flowers taught us last week. It's a coupling, she said, and she advised us: "Learn it off by heart, ladies! Listen for it in conversation – your own, other people's, on the radio – and as soon as you hear the 'not only', keep on listening because you will hear that it will be followed by 'but also'. And whenever you hear that coupling, call to your minds that it comes from the Latin, *'non solum… sed etiam'*. Now, say it all together, please? *Non solum… sed etiam.* Thank you!").

I interrupted myself. I wanted to explain that not only does she walk more quietly than most teachers, but also (there it is! *sed etiam*) she always closes the door very quietly as she enters. So she really keeps us on the lookout for when she comes into the classroom.

I've decided that she creeps in on purpose, closing the door so quietly and then standing so silently. I think it's her way of making us be ready for our lesson. I think it's part of the way she treats us like Ladies and not just girls.

Moreover (*autem*: we had to learn that one, too), she never has to stand there for very long 'cos you can always sense her presence somehow. You just gradually get a feeling that something's happened in the classroom, even if she doesn't say a word (which she doesn't). What happens is that as soon as the first person has noticed that she's come in, they'll immediately stop talking and they'll turn round properly towards the front and stand up. (We always have to stand up whenever a teacher comes into the classroom.) Then of course the others from that girl's group notice, too, and by the time they've stood up we'll all notice 'cos we'll hear the chairs scraping on the floor, so very quickly a ripple will go through the classroom until we're all standing. When we've done that, Miss Flowers will keep doing her standing, waiting. I've noticed that she always places her hands on either side of the chair, and she sort of lifts it and replaces it – silently, of course – beneath the teacher's desk in front of her. She'll just stand and stand and look straight in front of her, or sometimes her eyes will wander over the whole class until we have all listened to the quietness and nobody dares to make a squeak.

But one of the things I like about Miss Flowers is that she does all this without ever glaring – she only ever *looks*, not glares – and she's never ever given us a speech about what a shameful noisy lot we are. I like that.

She'll just stand there and when we've all gone hushed, she'll allow the pause to continue for as long as it takes for us to be admiring her inside ourselves, and also feel quite guilty for having not noticed her entrance. As soon as we're admiring her and feeling enough guilt, I think she can tell, almost as if she's got an invisible measurer so she knows all about us. At that moment she'll suddenly lift her head to one side and tilt it slightly, and you might be worried in case she's going to get cross but she surprises you 'cos instead of that her face will glint with a warm smile and she'll say gently, "Morning, ladies!" But she uses an unexpectedly cheerful voice, as if absolutely nothing bad has happened and we're all going to start the class with a clean sheet (as Mummy would say) and no guilt, and this is *our* lesson that she wants us to enjoy.

I like Miss Flowers.

Mummy uses glaring sometimes, if any of us have been really naughty. She does it so that I feel as if she has caught hold of me with her eyes, and she won't let go. I get quite frightened sometimes, and I feel very prickly inside and I always wish I could just creep away instead of having to stay standing in front of her. That's one of the things that I wish didn't happen, and that's one of the reasons why I'm so glad to have Uncle George. He knows that Mummy does the glaring and he is really nice to me about it. I've never told tales on Mummy; that's one way that Uncle George has proved to me he's so nice and so understanding.

I think it might have been the very first time I went to his house for tea that he first mentioned her glares, and he was extra-nice 'cos he didn't expect me to tell tales on Mummy but he talked about them. So I didn't feel I was being a traitor. He helped me to trust him more because of how much he really knew about how *I* feel. He must really understand what it's like to live in my home, and be the only girl, with Mummy being a bit strict (even though it's for my own good, which she always says), and with my brothers being bigger than me and teasing me.

Uncle George sometimes says to me, "You are such a good girl, Rose," and I look at him to see if he really means that, 'cos I do *want* to be good. I know God wants us to be good, and I want God to be pleased with me. My Sunday school teacher told us that when we get to heaven God will look at us and say, "Well done, good and faithful servant!"

That would be a very, very special thing to hear.

Oops, Miss Flowers has lifted up the textbook. She must be about to read a passage to us, so I ought to follow. What page are we on?

But while I look up the page, I'll quickly memorize whatever it is that makes Amanda look so lady-like. I must work out exactly what she's done. She's leaning forward slightly; her chair is a little distance away from her desk so there is space for her knees to be visible instead of underneath the desk. Her textbook is open on top and, although she's using the forefinger of one hand to follow the words, she's put her other hand under her chin. I think it must be the angle she's got her wrist under her chin that makes her look so elegant – or is it her arm? What *is* it? She's perched her elbow on her knee, then her forearm comes up towards her face and finally her hand is holding up her chin. Oh, but – aha, maybe this is her secret – her hand isn't cupped. She isn't leaning on the *palm* of her hand. She's holding her hand with her palm facing downwards, and her chin is leaning on the *back* of her hand, and her fingers are straight and pointing forwards such that we can all see her fingernails in a row. And her nails are very well shaped; she once told me that that's because she does manicuring. I still don't know how to do that, but I didn't dare say so to Amanda 'cos I knew that that would show me up as being not as grown up as she is, and silly for not having learned all the lady-like things she already knows.

....

GOODBYE PINK ROOM

Thinking of "manicuring" makes me remember about my manicure set that I once got from Aunty Vi for Christmas, and it was heart-shaped. Aunty Vi seems to know more about girls' things – women's things – than Mummy does, but she lives so far away that I hardly ever see her. And what I never told anyone about her manicure set was that when I opened the press-stud click and saw the different instruments that were in the set, I didn't know what to do with at least half of them. I never found out because, when there was nobody else in the house, I took it to Mummy to show her all the things. I was going to ask her what they were all for, but before I'd asked her anything, she waved her hand in a quick, sweeping movement and she said, "Oh, that thing!" as if it had been a very disappointing present (which I hadn't known that it was). Then she said, "Not only is it made of plastic, but also (*non solum... sed etiam*) that sort of thing is vanity. Sheer vanity. The best thing you can do is to give it away!"

I feel a bit guilty saying this, but I didn't give the manicure set away. I've still got it in a drawer in my dressing table. I keep it hidden safely underneath my socks and things, just in case Mummy finds it and in case she feels in the mood to give it to someone when I'm not there, and I couldn't rescue it.

One day I'll work out what all the things are in the set, and then I'll have nails like Amanda's, and then I'll be able to sit like her too and I'll look like a grown-up lady.

There's just one other thing that I'm thinking about my Latin lessons and I hope I can explain it but I don't know if I can find the right words. It's just that it was in Miss Flowers' lessons that I learned the whole rule about how things work in life – that it's when you do one thing, you probably also do another thing. *Non solum... sed etiam*. And what I'm trying to say is that I think that Miss Flowers might understand a little bit that with Uncle George...

... Oh dear, I don't know how to explain this properly...

… When I go out with Uncle George, I don't *only* have a nice time. When I go out with him, I don't realize this at the time when it's happening, but while I'm having a nice time with him understanding me, later on I sometimes feel sad, and that's when I realize that *also* I've felt other things as well as happy because of him understanding me.

I do *like* Uncle George understanding me, and I do *want* him to. But I'm just trying to say that I not only feel that happiness, but also I feel this funny-peculiar *un*happiness. I'm very sorry if that means that I am greedy for too much niceness, 'cos that makes me feel ashamed of myself. I'm only trying to work it out now; now that I'm telling my story – I'm thinking in the way I do when I sit up in my tree. I'm working out that I think I liked Miss Flowers for more than just one reason. I think that because she was the teacher who taught us to look out for *non solum… sed etiam*, then that means that she would be the person who might understand *me*.

I'm thinking more about Miss Flowers and how I feel when I am near her, for example when she calls us to come to her desk one at a time to get our marks for our homework. Whenever it's my turn, I feel sort of warm inside. I wouldn't ever tell anyone of course, but I like feeling that feeling, and I let myself feel it 'cos I prefer to concentrate on that while I'm at her desk, rather than to listen to her actual words as she goes over my homework.

Amanda has put her hand up again.

12

Trance

Sometimes a funny thing happens. It's as if I sort of wake up, even though I haven't been asleep. I just find that I'm somewhere, like on my branch up in the old oak tree, and I can't remember getting there. In fact, the only reason I know I'm there is that suddenly I hear Mummy calling, "Come *along*, Rose! I've been calling and calling. What do you think you're doing, just disappearing like that?!"

I have to sort of shake myself then, and pull myself together, and tear my mind away from wherever it has gone. While I'm climbing down, Mummy will keep talking. "Now come in at once. The meal's ready. Get those hands washed and sit down at the table…"

I really don't understand these things, and I get really sorry (which I don't think Mummy knows) because of not wanting to be a bad person.

I'm not up the tree now: I'm only writing about it, sitting at my desk that used to be Daddy's desk. But writing things down is making me see that the trouble comes when I try to have a very, very quick peep at one or two of the things that I don't want to think about, but that I do need to work out. I don't like not understanding, and how I feel lost sometimes.

But it never works. Everything is bigger than I can work out. 'Cos as soon as I have the tiniest little peep, I feel as if a huge wave of water comes up like the sea that swooshes in so fast that I've begun to drown before I've even realized that there's any water at all. Then I just feel a panic; a terrible panic. It's terror. It isn't calm or quiet or still. I just think, "Help! What can I do?" I think that's when I get lost, or I make myself go cold.

Mummy sounds so strict when she calls for me to "Get in here right now, my girl!" Her voice has a sort of rhythm: "Duh duh duh *duh duh* dit derr!" Her voice pierces the air. I hate that. Each word sounds like a staccato note.

The trouble is that when I've got lost I don't know how to "wake up". Well, Mummy does force me to. She shouts so clearly what I've got to do, and that startles me into getting myself down from where I've got stuck.

Maybe that actually helps me, even though I hate it so much. Maybe she helps me to "wake up".

I do know that I have to keep acting normally. I *have* to pull myself together. There isn't a choice. I *have* to do it.

13

Pressing the Buzzer

My headmistress's office has a very special bell fixed on to the side of her door. We're not allowed to knock on the door because we have to use the new bell instead. It's got a posh way of answering us when we go to see her because it lights up with the message that our headmistress chooses with how she wants to reply. I've come to her office so many times after school has ended that I've memorized how it all works.

When you first press the bell, a little white bulb inside the box lights up and that tells you that it knows you're there, so the headmistress knows that someone is waiting for her – wanting her – and then I know that she'll answer in a minute. Sometimes I get a bit nervous at that moment, in case I can't think of a good enough reason for having come to see her; but usually I'm not nervous 'cos I've thought of something to show her that I've read about, or something that I've discovered and I think she'd be pleased with me for noticing it (especially if nobody else has). But just sometimes – not very often – I stand there and a little bit of me hopes that she isn't going to be there. That only happens if I start to think that she might decide that my reason for coming to see her isn't quite important enough. It would be very terrible if she ever got tired of me coming to her; but I can't imagine that that would ever happen. I try to be very careful and be sure that she'll think I've come for a very good reason every time.

I don't know how often I come to see her, but maybe I come two or three times in a week. The reason I don't know this very well is that I don't always notice everything. It just happens. Quite often I suddenly just find that I've already pressed her bell and I'm standing there, and I'm waiting for her answer before I think properly about what I'm doing. It's as if I sort of "wake up" even though I haven't been asleep at all.

What happens is that at the end of school, when the bell goes, most people have their satchels packed so they're all ready to run up the hill to the bus stop so they can catch a bus before it gets terribly crowded. I don't get the bus 'cos I live so near to school, so I don't have to rush like all those people. Anyway, we're not supposed to scramble like ragamuffins who don't know how to behave: we're supposed to walk like ladies. We have teachers who lurk behind the doors, which are so narrow that people often push one another to hurry them up in their rush to get to the bus stop. If the teachers spy anyone pushing or if anyone goes through the door and allows it to swing behind them instead of holding it open politely, the teacher grabs hold of you and gives a long speech about how dangerous it is to allow a door to swing behind you because that could do terrible damage to someone's face. You get a detention straight away if you do that.

Anyway, I only see people rushing off towards their bus, or some of them walk down the hill to catch a train 'cos pupils come from a long way away to go to my school. But I'm left out of all the rushing, which is why I sometimes watch them and I see the classroom getting emptier and emptier until I might be the last person in the classroom. I don't have to rush 'cos if I leave school as soon as the lessons finish, I get home before anyone else in the family and I don't really like that 'cos it's a little bit lonely.

First of all I have to find the key that's hidden on a nail that Daddy put in a special place that he invented because he said that no burglar would look in that place. When I've put the key back (we always *have* to put it back, otherwise Mummy would tell us off terribly badly because of how irresponsible it would be to

GOODBYE PINK ROOM

let another member of the family be locked out), then I go into the house and it's completely silent. Actually sometimes I'm a bit silly 'cos I call, "Hello!" I know that there can't be anyone else there 'cos the back door was locked; but I shout "Hello!" very loudly 'cos if a burglar *was* there, he would hear me shouting "Hello!" and that would warn him that someone had come home, and he'd run away. So I feel a bit safer if I do that; but I don't tell anybody 'cos I know they'd all just laugh at me.

But one of the things I've started to do is to stay in school for a bit longer, and then I hope that our house won't be empty by the time I get home. Sometimes I make myself be late going home by going to the library. I quite like that because if my teachers see me they give me a smile 'cos they get pleased with me for using the library books to help with my homework. They don't know that it's not really because I'm doing my homework; it's only 'cos the library isn't so lonely as being at home on my own.

Another thing that I do to make myself be later arriving home is to stay in our classroom, and I look around at things there. I'm not really sure why I do that and sometimes I get frightened that maybe I'm being a bit nosey, like when I look at what people have scratched on their desks or what they've stored on the shelves in the classroom. The trouble is that I don't really know the reason why I stay there and I hope – I really hope – that it's not a bit naughty of me to do that. I'm not doing work. I'm not doing anything, really. I'm just being there.

And I think about things. If it's still early in the week I think about what's happened with Uncle George last Saturday, or if it's late in the week I think about what might happen next Saturday. I wish I didn't get reminded about that, but I can't help it: it just sits in my head. When I'm in the classroom I try to work out whether anyone else in my class might know anything about the things that he talks about, or the things that he does, or the things that he makes me do. I wonder if I can ask them what they would do if he did things with *them?* But nobody talks about the things that Uncle George does, so I don't think that *anyone* would know about those sorts of things. That makes me feel a bit more lonely because... well, I don't know why "because". I think – but I'm not very sure – that on the days when I think about those things and I can't work out why I feel lonely about it, I think that that's why I go to the headmistress's office and I see her, because that feels better than just thinking about things on my own.

I always feel very happy when I see the green bit on her door lighting up around the word "Enter". I feel welcomed, and warmed, and I'm glad to think that the headmistress wants to talk with me. But after I've stood waiting for a little while and nothing lights up, I begin to wonder if she's gone out or something disappointing like that. While I'm waiting I never know what colour it's going to be when it lights up, and what the black letters will say: that stays as a secret until the headmistress presses her special button that must be fixed on her desk somewhere I think. I try not to get too disappointed when her reply makes the orange bulb light up surrounding black letters that say, "Wait". I always do wait, even if I have to wait for a very long time, 'cos I always look forward to seeing her and to talking to her. I always feel a bit better when we've spoken to one another, which is why it's always worth waiting in the corridor for her.

The worst time is whenever the light flashes on red, and that makes me sad 'cos the red light surrounds the black letters of the long word, "Engaged". I hate when it says "Engaged" 'cos that means that she doesn't want to see me, no matter what's wrong or how much I wanted to see her. When that happens, I always walk away from her door very slowly. Actually, sometimes I don't even go away immediately: sometimes I stay outside her door, just to feel the feeling of what it means to be a little bit closer to her.

I like sitting in the headmistress's office because of the warm feeling I have inside me. I don't mean the warm feeling from the

GOODBYE PINK ROOM

fire, although her room does have a gas fire that always makes a friendly "pop, pop" noise, and it's lovely and warm when I'm allowed to sit next to the hearth at the side of the fire. Sometimes the headmistress has a cup of tea, and a few times she has asked me if I would like to join her, so that helps me to know that I'm not a nuisance to her. I wouldn't like to be a nuisance, but I think that she must like me coming to visit her 'cos otherwise she wouldn't offer me the drink, which must be her way of asking me please if I will stay? I think maybe the headmistress might be a little bit lonely herself, and that must be why she's nice to me and that must be why, when I go to visit her after school, she presses the switch that's green and says "Enter".

It's not very often that she has pressed the red "Engaged" button to reject me or to keep me away. I think that she must only do that when she's extra busy – probably when she's got lots of reports to write, like Mummy who gets very busy. When Mummy's got so many reports for her pupils in her school and she has all her marking, she hasn't got time for us children and we just don't understand at all. I think that my headmistress must feel the same as Mummy and that must be what happens when she makes me go away. I'm sorry for saying this bit, but I get a bit sad when I see the red light saying "Engaged". Just a very little bit.

I walk away very, very slowly, and while I am walking I stare down at my shoes, because I'm watching each step as my legs take me further and further away from her warm office. Still, I cheer myself up when that happens at the beginning of the week because of a secret reason. I don't mind watching my shoes when they are shiny, which they are whenever Daddy has polished them. He polishes all of the shoes for all of us children every Sunday evening so that they are ready for the new week, he says. He lines them up on the newspaper when he's done them all, and the whole kitchen smells of lovely polish and I feel very cared for by Daddy.

So if I have to stare at my shoes and they are nicely polished, I can make myself feel happier 'cos I can admire how very shiny they look, and I can think about how kind Daddy is and that helps me not to mind if the headmistress had to send me away. If I think about my shoes while I'm walking along looking down at them, seeing how well polished they are as I watch them stepping forwards one after another taking me home, then they can help me not to feel unhappy. Granny says it's important to remember what a very lucky girl I am to have such loving parents who care for me so much, and I think she must be right 'cos I've noticed that some children's shoes haven't been polished at all and they look very scruffy, which must mean that they're not loved properly.

Poor them.

14

Shutting the Door

I'm just thinking about things.

I'm thinking about the toy cupboard in the boys' room. It has that long door, which some people might believe leads into another whole room. Or they might think it would take them into another world, like Narnia. Our cupboard isn't as magic as Narnia but I sometimes think that it is a little bit magic, and this is why. Our toys seem to sort of get changed in there. What happens is, when you put them away you think that they're a bit boring and old. But if you leave them in there for a long enough time, then when you take them out suddenly they seem to be more exciting, even like a whole new toy!

So that's why I say that the cupboard has a little bit of magic that changes the toys.

I've been putting everything that happens with Uncle George into a cupboard like this one. I'm leaving it there, so that everything will get changed like the toys get changed. Everything will become all right. At least, I hope so. I hope that it only needs enough time.

But I'm getting worried 'cos my memory-cupboard has got more and more full. I've had to try harder and harder to get the door closed each time I've added another Saturday's Happenings. It's not all fitting properly any more.

Just get today's stuff in and close the door fast, Rose!

But it won't fit! I'll have to try to see if... Don't look! You mustn't look! Ram things in and slam the door. Push harder if it won't shut. It's got to go! No, you can't sort it out 'cos that would mean you'd have to touch one of the things that you've already squeezed in and you mustn't touch anything – you *mustn't*. You mustn't take anything out in case it bites you. Now, just get today's in, just get it *in*. Don't even think about anything else. It's only today's that needs to go in and quick, quick! You must get it on the shelf in case somebody comes! They might see!

So now then, hold things there with your left hand – gently, carefully now… keep it from toppling out, hold it still, and very gingerly, with your right hand, feel for the shape of the door behind you… that's it, there; now get enough of a hold to push it shut. Quick! Slam it all the way shut and hold it there till everything that might fall over has settled and forgotten it was about to fall and then it'll stay in there. Stay… Stay…

I'm sitting on the floor with my back to the cupboard door, almost breathless after the effort of stuffing all my memories into the darkness behind me. I'm a bit frightened that if I move away, the cupboard door might fall open by mistake. I couldn't bear it if that happened.

I wish I didn't have all this stuff. Because the trouble is, I haven't sorted everything out, even though I've spent time in the tree. I am always trying to work everything out, and I always feel that if only I tried hard enough, I would be able to understand. But at the same time, I also have to forget everything. And I just don't know how I can do both things…

Before I walk away or take my weight away from leaning hard against the door to make sure that it doesn't burst open, I'll have to find something to press against it, instead of my own body. I'm searching around me: what can I do? I have to leave – I can't stay here all my life on sentry duty. I have school to go to and meals and Brownies and church aı d swimming and cycling with Daddy and horse-riding and all the things I do, that everybody does. I simply can't stay here all my life!

So what can I do about this stupid door to stop it falling open? I'll have to find something else – something heavy… There, perhaps that heavy chair. I could jam that against my cupboard door…

And so I moved the furniture of my life, and there will have been something "odd" about my behaviour at times, if only people had noticed. Other people's politeness or respect for me will, quite unwittingly, have helped to draw a veil over the truth. Kindness, respect, and courtesy are very forgiving. But I developed a ritual in which I became both a sergeant major and a junior soldier, issuing the instructions and having to obey them. The sergeant major insisted on immediate obedience, so that nothing in the cupboard could be disturbed. "Don't look back." "Live today." "Keep your eyes ahead."

Unsurprisingly, the habit persists. I am an adult now, but whenever I become pressured or afraid, I adopt the same mechanism subconsciously. I tell myself I must do as I say, immediately. The more I understand my history, the more gently I can recognize (and then change) when I'm chanting to myself, dictating to myself, behaving in a way that is not consistent with my "normal" adult self.

Opening the door is a different story. It is dangerous because what I buried has the potential to overwhelm me completely. I keep the door closed – with one exception. Only recently did I realize that God actually addressed this issue of our closed doors. "See! I stand at the door and knock. If anyone hears My voice and opens the door, I will come in…"[2]

So I have promised that if He knocks, I will open it. The purpose, then, will not be to wallow in history, but to allow Jesus to come in. That brings hope, and healing: the very fragrance of God.

But I am jumping ahead.

---

2   Revelation 3:20 NLV.

15

The Raindrop

It's raining again today and I've decided to concentrate very hard on one single drop of rain.

I've turned my head so that I can look at this drop properly and carefully. If he asks me why I've turned my head away from him, I'll be able to say that I haven't turned it *away*, I've turned it *towards* the thing I'm watching. He won't understand that, and that's 'cos he doesn't know I'm watching it. He thinks – well, I don't really know what he thinks, but I am sure he doesn't know that I'm thinking about the raindrop and I like being able to do something that he doesn't know. He thinks he knows all about me and he doesn't.

He thinks he's giving me fun.

What he's doing isn't fun. Well, not for me it isn't but I couldn't say so to him.

Oh dear. He says he's very proud of the way I'm growing up, and he's so understanding every time about how no one in my family ever talks about things like this, and we laugh about that. He once said that he betted that Mummy never talks about "snogging" and of course he was right. I felt very grown up 'cos I knew the word "snogging" and I didn't have to ask him what it meant. I knew that it meant putting faces together and touching lips and holding them there for a very long time. I did that once with a boy at my old school one day last year, when three of the boys and I all went round to a little alley-way round the back after school. They each wanted to kiss me and they said they'd stand in a line and close their eyes and I must choose who I liked the best and I could kiss that one. But when they shut their eyes I didn't trust they'd *keep* them shut, so I didn't kiss any of them the first time and when I said I'd finished they all said, "But you haven't kissed anyone!" so I knew they must have peeped. That was my way of finding out, and I was right.

Then they promised they wouldn't peep next time, and they shut their eyes again, and that time I didn't dare to kiss the one that I *really* liked best and I kissed the one I thought would be hurt if I didn't choose him. Then the others opened their eyes and then we all argued about the rules again and I can't remember all about it 'cos what I remember most is that I wished I had kissed the one I really liked the best and I knew I'd been silly. Anyway, we played the game again and when I kissed the second one he did the snogging 'cos he held me very tightly to him with his arms right round me, so when our mouths touched at the lips I couldn't get away and that was called snogging. My neck ached a bit 'cos he was taller than I was and it went on for longer than a normal kiss and I didn't know why people on films thought that was so good but I felt very grown up.

So when Uncle George first talked about the snogging I knew it was a bit boring but I didn't say so in case that made him think badly of me or be disappointed in me.

I'm not going to think about kissing or anything he's doing at this moment.

He told me I'm not very good at the snogging which is why he's got to teach me how to do it better, otherwise I won't grow up to be a proper lady that nice men will want to marry. You've got to kiss properly to marry and it's a special knack – he says it's an art – which is quite complicated. It must be that I'm not good enough 'cos that's why I've got to have so many lessons.

But when Uncle George speaks, he sometimes has a little blob of white in the middle of his bottom lip and… and… and I hate that. It makes me think about something I can't think about.

I feel horrible inside.

I'm terribly frightened.

Whenever I see his blob moving, it makes me remember about different kissing, which is completely horrible and makes me feel I'm choking. Then I get his white stuff in my mouth and I'll have swallowed it which makes me feel so sick that I even get frightened I might actually be sick. I never want to do that other sort of kissing, ever again.

Help, help; I mustn't remember anything about that at all. My mind is falling, falling down the slide, and I don't know how to stop it. Oh yes, there's the raindrop. I'm thinking about the raindrop.

This one raindrop has been in the same place for a long time. It's hanging there, not on the windscreen in front of me, but on the window of the door beside me. There's a line of silver metal on the door to separate the main window of my door from the little triangular side-window next to the windscreen. The triangular window has got a hook for undoing it, which I like. I think it's very sweet and I sometimes ask if I can open the window just so I can press the knob and enjoy turning the little latch and then pushing the little window open.

The raindrop that I'm looking at is on the main window right beside the metal piece. Maybe the drop is sort of sheltering from the wind 'cos maybe the metal gives it shelter. Maybe that's why the same drop of rain has been there for such a long time without it dripping down or being blown down like the others.

I'm playing a game of guessing when it'll start to roll down the window. That helps me to not think about what Uncle George is doing.

I nearly thought about Uncle George just then and suddenly I thought that the raindrop looked like a teardrop, and I very nearly had a tear coming into my eye but I managed to stop it quickly enough 'cos it would be absolutely terrible if I ever got a tear while Uncle George is teaching me to be grown up. That would be more proof that I'm silly and I so don't want to be that. I hate when anyone says I am and I try very, very hard not to be. I even pray and ask God to help me to grow up and not to be silly. So I must be quick and think about the raindrop.

The raindrop that I'm looking at now is a little bit like a friend to me. It's only a thing, I know, but it's like a friend because it's something for me to think about. It keeps staying there no matter what happens and I like that, although it might start rolling down soon and then it will have gone away forever. It doesn't make any sound – it's just there, which is what makes it a little bit like a teddy. Adults and teachers say that teddies are "only a thing". I don't know if they've never found out how much a teddy can be a friend, or if they did find out when they were children but now they've forgotten. Or maybe you get taught how to forget these things when you learn to be a teacher. I'm not sure.

I've started staring extra-hard at the drop 'cos I need to concentrate on it so hard that I think about nothing else at all; and now that I'm doing that I can see that the middle of it is brighter than the outside of it, and it's brighter than the bushes that are outside the car. When I make my eyes concentrate extra-hard on that *one* drop, just on its own, I can see that it's got a picture of the clouds in it. That must be why it shows up against the bushes as being white. The whiteness on the drop is the white of the clouds in the sky. This raindrop seems to bring some of the sky down to the earth 'cos I can see the white cloud of the sky is inside the drop.

Some people say that heaven is in the sky, or when they talk about heaven they look up at the sky. But I don't believe that 'cos I think that if heaven was up there then an aeroplane would bump into it. Anyway I think heaven must be a place you can't see, where people live without being seen. That's why you can't see people going there when they die.

But when I'm thinking about things and trying not to think about sore things or difficult things that I wish weren't happening to me, and when I'm trying to keep as cheerful as when Daddy says he loves his Darling Daughter who is very smiley and everyone says is full of fun… when I feel sad inside but I'm trying to keep cheerful outside, then I sometimes wish that heaven was a place that's so real that you could bump into it.

And now that I've seen that this raindrop has a cloud on it, and the raindrop is down here right beside me on the window – here, right beside where my head is – I don't completely believe this but I'm going to pretend that I believe that this raindrop with a cloud is like a little bit of heaven. This little bit of heaven is sitting very near to me, and it's been there for so long that it must have seen everything that Uncle George's been doing and what I won't look at, and it knows, so that's what makes it even more of my friend.

I hope that God's seen too, except some grown-ups say that God turns His face away from you if you're too naughty. But I don't want to be naughty and I don't really believe that God turns His face away because I know how much He loves me. And He must know that I love Him, too, and I hope this isn't naughty, and Uncle George says it isn't and…

I mustn't cry, so I must must must stop thinking what I nearly started thinking then.

What I'm going to think is this. Here is a raindrop that hasn't rolled down the window. It is a raindrop with a cloud (if you stare at it very, very hard, which I am).

That means that this raindrop has come from heaven.

That means that this is a sign that heaven is here.

Heaven has come to earth. It shows me that I am safe because heaven is here.

You're always safe in heaven.

16

Lamp-Posts

I'm being driven past lamp-post after lamp-post. I'm not looking at them, but I know that they're there because the orange from each one makes the darkness glow.

I don't want there to be any lamp-posts at all. I'm not ready for them. That's why I put the blankets over my head, 'cos I'm trying to not hear what lamp-posts mean, but the light still pushes its way through the blankets.

Each lamp-post makes an announcement, silently but very loudly. You're one lamp-post nearer to home now.

The car makes a shwooshing sound as it drives past each one, and that swoosh says the same message. One more again. And again. You're on the way back. With each lamp-post mile you pass, each mile you travel, you come nearer to the place where the motto will be (and Rose, you will *have* to believe these words with Absolutely, Do-Not-Contradict-Me, Undeniable, This-is-Fact certainty): All over now. It's all over.

Or sometimes, as he says, "Finished now." Or, "We're finished now."

Rose, you've got to listen to this. Nothing has happened that's out of the ordinary. You're just a normal teenager with kind Uncle George; you've had a treat of a day. He's taken you out and given you what most girls would have enjoyed, and loved, and they would have been truly grateful. Not like you. Now, pull yourself together! The very *least* you can do is be grateful!

And the closer you get to home, the sooner you will need to put on your smiling face with your bright smile. ("Rose has such a lovely smile!") And you'll have to thank him.

Very soon the lamp-posts will have counted down to nil, and I will have arrived.

Oh no! No no no! How can I switch? How can I change the points?

I shall have to tell my head – and the whole of the rest of me – to get up from these blankets on the back seat. I'll have to face the world. Put on a brave face. I'll have to enter the world where the only way of coping is to pretend. I'll have to put away anything that doesn't fit together with nice Uncle George, with my nice supportive family, with what Daddy and Mummy say about me, Rose, being their "Darling Daughter".

I'll have to force myself to raise my eyes and look into Uncle George's face and I'll have to give him a speech. Sometimes, when I get out of the car and just before I have to say all these things, I can feel that I've got a frown on my face. A puzzled frown.

I'll have to hide that. I'll have to look so sincere that Mummy is convinced when I say, with her listening, making sure I say it properly: "Thank you, Uncle George. Thank you for a lovely time."

I feel sick even thinking about this. My stomach is turning, churning, rejecting. Why did nobody see that this veneer of politeness needed only a tiny pinprick and its bubble would have burst and the air would have evaporated, leaving the truth lying on the ground of the moor to which he'd taken me, screaming its wretched, terrifying, terrorizing truth?

Occasionally when we'd rung the doorbell and my mother received me home, we would stand – all three of us – either on the front doorstep or a little further in, within the warmer entrance hall of our house, and I'd be asked further questions. My mother put so very much energy into educating me, all for love of me. She didn't want to let me down. And yet as I recall the sorts of questions that she believed to be good, I almost despair because of what she didn't know – couldn't know, and I couldn't say.

"So, where have you been? Can you show me on the map?" My mind would spin and split again: part of me desperate to disappear upstairs to my pink room to greet it once more, to check on all the familiar signs of security, to see if it was all the same, to feel whether or not it would give me the welcome home for which I craved. Another part of me would stand there as if I were in school at the front of the whole class, my geography teacher having pulled me out from my desk to stand me on display before all the others, firing questions at me, forcing me to see that I didn't come up to the standard required.

"Where, exactly, did you go? Which bit of the moor: did you go to the north, south, east or west?" And I'd tremble with fear, because I hadn't taken that part of my brain on the outing with Uncle George.

"Out in the country," I wanted to say. I thought that might have given enough of a clue that I had been lost, and not just geographically. I had got lost in my mind and my emotions. He took me to where there were no landmarks; to where I saw nothing that would help me to find the same place again or my way home.

As I stood in the hallway of home at the end of the trip, I had my mother's face waiting for the answer, "Where were you?" and my mind simply flooded with feelings, and not with good answers to geography questions. Inside, I would shout at her: "For heaven's sake! Where we were was of no importance at all!"

Yet here we clashed, because it was so important to her that I knew my geography; whereas for me, the important things were on a different plane altogether. I could have described the place Uncle George had parked his car; I could have said that it felt scary to have bumped our way down such a disused track. I could have told of the bleak outlook, and that I'd looked for villages but had seen none – not even a farm to give me comfort of human habitation nearby.

I could have spoken of the bareness outside on the moor. And that word "bareness" would have had me shuddering. And more…

But the more these thoughts flashed through my mind, the more they caused me to stumble, and become silent. And the more silent I became, the less I felt able to get out of this dreadful situation. So I'd look around in dismay and confusion and look for the first opportunity to excuse myself and race upstairs to my room – my pink room. Oh, I had to get away from that hall and get up to my room…

But as the polite conversation continued, I'd be stuck with where my thoughts last got caught, which, on this occasion, was the thought of my skirt. I'd allowed myself to think – by mistake, I'd somehow let this happen – to think of my turquoise skirt, flared with seams roughly sewn. It was the first skirt I'd ever bought for myself, without my mother. I'd taken the bus to Exeter and had seen it while rummaging purposefully through the display of Sale Goods, and there it was, looking so grown up: a flared mini-skirt. And I was so proud of it, and of myself in it. I had chosen it. And I could be so pleased that I had found a cheap one that was nice – it didn't look cheap. I hadn't noticed the roughly sewn seams and even if I had, I didn't want to care. That skirt was my grown-up skirt, my "I've got taste, I'm a big girl now" skirt.

And then, horror of horrors, first time on and he had made me feel so horrid underneath; tingly and horrid. How could I have let him? Why didn't I keep my legs so tightly together that he couldn't push his hand to where he did? How did I ever let him in? And feel grown up?

I hated myself.

Was it because his arm was round me and I felt loved?

Something in his gaze was wrong, but I didn't know what it was.

17

Goodbye Car

Goodbye, car.

Goodbye, nice hugs.

It's time for me to go inside now.

Goodbye, assurances that I was a good girl.

It's time to go in and see Mummy. I wish I didn't have to do something really good before Mummy sounds as pleased with me as Uncle George does when I'm on these trips. I have to get good marks at school; I'll have to come top of the class; I'll have to win the cup in tennis; I'll have to get a distinction in my music exam; wouldn't it be a shame if I only got a merit? And I know it's only because she loves me – she does say that, and so does Daddy, and I'm very lucky to have loving parents – but it's just that sometimes I feel as if I just can't be good enough. With Uncle George, I don't have to do anything before he says I'm good. But at home Mummy says, "I know you can do it. Wouldn't it be nice for you to see how well you've done? Just try a little bit harder, and you may even find an extra little something on top of your pocket money; a surprise for doing so well."

Uncle George! I don't want to go in! I don't want to leave you!

You've got to get up, Rose, and go in. You've got to say hello; you'll have to be a helpful girl; to set the table; to work hard for school; you must remember to be polite and never do things like making crumbs or speaking with your mouth full. You must be a good girl.

Oh help, help, what can I do if I can't?

. . . .

Goodbye, understanding smiles. Goodbye, promises to help me to grow up nicely. Goodbye for now. I'll see you again and I'll listen and hear and drink and feel the niceness of that.

Oh! I don't want to say goodbye. Even if Uncle George does things that I don't like! When I shut the car door I'll shut out of my mind the horrid things. And when I go in, I'll carry inside the nice things that he gives me, to help me all through the week.

Goodbye, someone who said I was special.

Passage of Time (2)

Several years
An escalation of events
Being caught like a fly in a spider's web,
like prey with transparent thread
spun delicately around me

18

Goodbye Again, Pink Room

I'm standing in my room and I've been standing and staring, and staring, but I've got to stop that now because it's nearly time again.

So it's time to say goodbye.

Goodbye, pink room.

Goodbye, daintiness.

I don't have my old teddy or my nice doll any more, so I can't say goodbye to them. They've been put away 'cos Mum said I've grown out of "teddies and dollies" (she used the baby words so I'd know how childish I would be if I even thought about applying – please – to be allowed to keep them for hugging, or talking to).

I wonder where I'll be going today?… Oh, I must stop myself from asking that. I'm not there yet.

I don't want to go!

I've got to go.

Goodbye, cupboard door with teddy and dolly that I'm too grown up to talk to. I'm whispering into the crack beside the door-handle now: I'll be back before tonight.

But what will have happened to me by then? What might he have done?

I don't want to go, but I've got to.

What will happen today?

Is it my fault that things go wrong?

Might something happen that stops me being able to smile? Might that time be today? Oh, help, help, what can I do if that happens?

It's nearly time. My wind-up alarm clock inside my heart is tick-tocking, pushing the hands towards the time he'll come and get me.

He's coming to get me. His hands will get me.

I've managed to stop myself from thinking about anything – everything – nearly everything – ever since last time but now that I'm going again, suddenly it's all flooding back…

What can I do to get ready to go? How can I "prepare"?

No; I mustn't panic. I must be calm. Everything's fine. I'm not "there" yet. I'm just saying goodbye…

Goodbye, desk.

I'm just staring now, staring and staring and not moving at all.

Goodbye, room.

Nice, pink room.

I still want to have a nice, dainty room… a pink room…

But I have grown out of child things now; so that must mean that I'm too old for toys and for baby pink. I've changed. And things have changed.

There is my Bible, on the top of the pile. Oh, what a comfort that keeps being! So many promises; so much assurance that God knows, and cares. Thank You, Father, for caring like a Daddy, and extra-thank You that You are such a good Friend to me, and thank You that nowadays I've come to know You better. I really love You, Lord.

But please, God, please… I know You've heard me ask this before, but please can You help me to feel You today? I know that You see everything, and I do trust Your promise that nothing's too hard for us. It's just that it's much easier to trust if I can feel You "there" – You know – in the middle of everything with Uncle George. Because when I can't see You or feel You, I get more frightened and sometimes I want to cry from loneliness. Just accidentally cry, that is.

Lord, I'm a bit muddled. Thank You for understanding when I can't explain. Thank You most of all that I know I belong to You and I still know that in the middle of everything.

Goodbye for now, Bible.

It's nice that I can't say goodbye to You, God, because You do stay with us even when we can't feel You.

I don't like saying goodbye.

19

The Silence

I must have become practised in saying that sort of goodbye. I hated every time I went out with Uncle George and developed a little ritual of parting with everything familiar in my room. One of the things that's happened since I started telling my story is that the old loathing has crept back, unbidden and unwanted, so that nowadays – thirty-five years on – I'll be on my way out and I'll suddenly find myself in a pickle that I would call "ridiculous" or "unnecessary"; quite out of character. My mood will become tinged with tension so that, instead of my feeling the excited anticipation I associate with going out, my mood will suddenly sabotage me, catching me unawares because my "goodbye" becomes tinged with apprehension.

With the benefit of hindsight, I have come to wonder if I absorbed into my every goodbye a sense of foreboding; an unspoken confusion and grief as I parted with teddy or my yellow-dressed dolly. Neither of them corrected me (of course!) – I was a child, learning on my own with only my toys to "teach" me. Perhaps I traced my finger along the line of teddy's mouth so many times that his black, stitched-up silence travelled through my forefinger, trickling up the very nerve fibres to my brain until it became imprinted indelibly on my mind.

Why did I keep saying these silent goodbyes, anyway?

Was there really no way that I could have told my parents? I knew they loved me. However much I used to quake at the thought of making Mum cross, I didn't doubt that she loved me.

I'm beginning to see that the web that entwined me had also been spun around my parents. They had no reason to question what Uncle George did. He was known in the community as a kindly gentleman. Maybe my parents were so helped by his generosity and encouraged by his thoughtfulness that they were blinded to any distorted motives he may have had.

But if I didn't go directly to my parents, what about Miss Marshall? Or Miss Flowers? I stood at her desk for long enough trying to derive comfort from being near her: could I not have spoken up? Whispered? Hinted? Alluded to the fact that all was not well?

Recently, someone proposed to me something I had never contemplated as a child. "Rose," she said, "can you take yourself back in your mind's eye, so you are standing beside Miss Flowers' desk, just as you used to do? Just suppose she somehow sensed from your non-verbal communication that something was wrong; suppose she guessed that behind your friendly smile you were actually quite distressed? What if she had sat you down and led you, kindly, gently, to say a very little… enough for her to realize that Uncle George was interfering inappropriately? If she'd have taken you seriously, and had accompanied you to see the headmistress, and if, together, they had begun to set the procedures in motion… They would have been the ones to contact your parents, so they would have explained what you couldn't say for yourself… can you picture them helping you like this? And then of course the child protection people would have come in to help, and maybe the police as well…"

I didn't hear any more. I couldn't bear to imagine the scene, even as an adult. I covered my ears and screamed a (silent) scream of "Stop! No! This is dreadful!" The thought of standing in front of the headmistress was intolerable. And as for anyone "explaining" to my parents or – worse – the police, this was completely unthinkable! I went cold all over. I froze. I stood speechless, taken back to my confused child state. How could the unspeakable have been spoken? "Explained"?

GOODBYE PINK ROOM

Thus, my silence was not a strategy. It was not a choice. It was a simple inevitability.

20

Happenings

I can't bear what is happening.

Can't.

But I have learned that I can make myself go silent inside my head and, when I do that, then that makes there be no words, and then that means there won't be anything. Not anything. Just nothingness. Whiteness. And that will be good.

It's not raining today and there are no raindrops for me to concentrate on. I remember one day when I watched one raindrop right beside me, and I saw a white cloud inside it, and that was like seeing heaven.

But there is no raindrop today, so I can't see anything of heaven.

I can't even tell myself that heaven is right next to me.

Anyway, so much is happening, and I so nearly feel as if I'm going to burst. My mind is spinning and spinning.

I'm making whiteness come into my head now, immediately.

I must make everything be whiteness.

Nothingness.

Blankness.

I can only do this if I be very quiet.

Completely quiet.

Silent.

I've got to make my whole mind go blank.
Everything must go away.
Don't think, Rose.
Even if I say, "Don't think", I'm still thinking.
I've *got* to stop thinking.
I mustn't think at all.
Don't think.

Hush…

I'm concentrating on blankness

I spun down

I can't talk

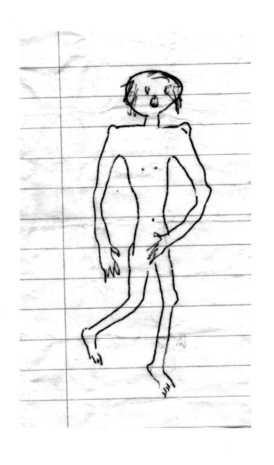

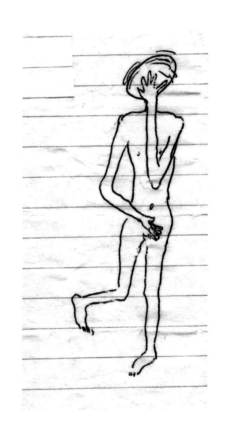

21

Daddy's Cushion

Something's happened!

I'm sure something's happened!

I feel so sore, I feel as if my insides have been completely ripped and torn.

What if they have been?

What's happened?

Oh, help, I just mustn't think about what it is. Everything is all so completely terrible now.

How will I get out of the car when we get home?

No, I can't think so far ahead. I must just get through this moment, right now. Like I did when… when…

… well, it was as if the whole *world* exploded.

God, please! Please! I need You! This is so sore, so very sore. And I can't tell anyone because of what it was, and no one would ever ask about this sort of thing because of how rude it is. It must all be my fault but… oh, what can I *do?*

I'm so frightened. Please, God, please mend me, especially the inside of me that feels as if he pressed…

… *No!* I must keep calm. Everything's all over now. It's like history. It's all over so there's no need to think about the past.

I would stop thinking about it except for whatever is happening to me now. At least, it's not exactly happening *to* me. Nothing's happening *to* me any more. But something's happening *in* me, and I don't know what, 'cos there'll be nothing to see, 'cos it wasn't like that.

· ·

Everything's gone all wrong. And I don't know what it is.

And because of what I don't know, I really wish I could have something... just this one thing that I'm remembering from when I was younger.

I know the soreness is because of the very terrible thing from him, from today. I have just absolutely got to forget all about it, and I can never, ever tell anyone about it because of how awful it was. I've sometimes thought that other things were bad, but today was completely different.

It really was the whole world that exploded, and it happened inside me. And fireworks went off; only, instead of just sparks coming out of the rockets, there were nails, and knives, and all sorts of sharp things that felt as if they were cutting the inside of me. They were hurting me very, very badly, and it would have been all right if they could have killed me and then it would have stopped.

I wish I could be in heaven 'cos this would all be over. But instead I've got to manage, somehow, with this terrible, dreadful thing that must be secret.

Mum must never ever know, 'cos I'm sure she'd believe him that it was my fault.

How can I manage with me being so sore, as if some of the fireworks are still exploding a little bit?

I wish I had the special cushion that I used to sit on when Daddy took me out on his bike. It doesn't look like a special cushion: it's just an old pink one from the kitchen. But the thought of this cushion reminds me of how I always felt when I used to sit on it. It's Daddy's cushion.

Daddy's cushion is very fluffy and it plumps up (that's Granny's word for what we have to do to all the cushions on the sofa. "Plump up the cushions!" she says, and it doesn't matter whether we're in her house or ours, she still tells us what to do and we have to "plump up the cushions" every night before we go to bed). Anyway this cushion plumps up very well, and it goes all

GOODBYE PINK ROOM

fat and comfortable. I like this cushion more than anyone in the family, which I would never tell my brothers 'cos I wouldn't want them to stop me from having it when I wanted it. But I know why I like it so much. It's one of my secrets.

The reason I like it is that I used to be given it for something that I never saw happen for any of my brothers. What happened was – oh, sigh, I'm dreaming about it now…

Daddy is taking me with him on his bike, and I'm being allowed to ride on the crossbar with the cushion. I like doing this very, very much 'cos when I'm on the bike and he's pedalling along, he sort of hugs me when he might not even know. I'm not sure whether he knows or not. But I know. I know 'cos I can see his arms which come down from his shoulders to the handlebars and I'm in between them and I can feel them. I feel very safe and I know I'm completely protected 'cos he's got his arms on either side of me and that means that I couldn't possibly fall off. Or if we both fell off by accident (which I don't think we ever would anyway, because Daddy's a very good cyclist), if we did fall off I couldn't get hurt 'cos Daddy's arms would be round me and they'd stop me from getting hurt. That's how I know how safe I always am.

Sometimes Mummy worries about me going on Daddy's bike, and she stands at the back door just as we're setting off, and that spoils my very excited feeling when my tummy's moving around with excitement 'cos I'm going with Daddy, and Daddy's *chosen* me to go with him (that's the best bit). Anyway sometimes Mummy will come to the door to wave us off and she'll say, "Will Rose be safe, perched there?" She can't know how safe I am 'cos I've got Daddy's arms round me all the time, no matter what. I've even got his arms there when he's turning left or turning right 'cos he doesn't even take his arm away from being round me to do his hand signals. Instead he tells me what he's going to do ahead of time and then he says, "So you put your arm out,

Rose!" and I put my arm out very, very straight and I make my hand be very straight too, right up to the ends of my fingertips – very straight – so that anyone will see which way we're going to go on Daddy's bike. I think even the strictest policeman would smile at us if he watched Daddy and me cycling along 'cos he'd see how very well Daddy's taught me to do arm signals on your bike. So that's another reason why I feel very safe.

I think that Mummy can't know how safe Daddy and I are, and that means that she doesn't know everything even though she does know an awful lot.

Anyway, every time we go out and before we actually set off, Daddy picks up this cushion. I think he must know that this is the best cushion for making the crossbar of his bike be the best-padded. I watch him go round all the chairs that are pushed under the kitchen table and he looks and looks until he finds *this* cushion – the one that plumps up the biggest and the best. Then he tucks it under his arm and gets his bike and he places the cushion on the crossbar. And he doesn't just plonk it on any old how; he takes great care and his mouth makes a sound that's as if he's sort of saying "Ski", which he does whenever he's concentrating. He plumps up the cushion and he curls the edges around and tries to make it go round the crossbar two times so that it's the most comfortable for me that he can possibly make it. And I watch him 'cos I know that he always does all this specially for me, so that I'll be comfortable and so the crossbar is "not too hard for your bones". (That's what Daddy says.)

I stand on the step outside the kitchen, waiting, and I know not to say anything 'cos that rushes him, so I wait until he's stopped fiddling and then he'll say, "There you are, dear!" And he'll smile nicely to me, as a way of saying that he wants me to get on now.

Then he puts his left arm out to receive me with a sort of hug, and I don't need him to help me 'cos I can manage to get onto the cushion without any help but I like him putting his arm out 'cos he's a real gentleman, my Daddy. And when I'm on he'll say, "Are you all right there, dear?" and I'll say, "Yes, I'm fine, thank you, Daddy!" and I can feel my tummy getting all excited 'cos I'm going out on Daddy's bike, safely held between his arms.

When we start riding we usually go up the hill on our road first and the hill keeps going for so far that Daddy will start to get puffed. I know this 'cos my ears are so near to his chest that I can hear his breathing and I can tell how puffed he is. If I haven't got a hat on I can feel his breath on the back of my head as well, but usually I have to wear a hat 'cos Mummy doesn't want me to catch my death of cold.

Sometimes Daddy talks to me a little bit, although usually he doesn't talk and I don't talk either. Instead, I just enjoy riding between his arms and I have a smile inside myself. I think that Daddy probably has a smile inside himself too, 'cos although he doesn't say things I think he's happy. Sometimes he sings and sometimes we both laugh 'cos we both sing, and we make descants together. He says I'm good at singing but Miss Marshall won't let me be in the choir, which must mean she doesn't think I'm good enough. But I like singing on Daddy's bike, and he tells me that I've got to keep to the tune while he does a different tune that he says is called a harmony, and my tune is called the melody, he says. And sometimes we do a round, which means that I start first and I have to keep going and then he starts after me, and that's with songs like "Frère Jacques".

Sometimes we don't talk and we don't sing, but we just ride, and if there's a long hill downhill he asks if I'm ready to go fast and he doesn't pedal but we just sing a very long "Weeeeeee!" all the way down. But Daddy knows that I don't like going too fast, and he says I can always shout "Slow down!" if I get a bit frightened, which I do even though I don't know why, but he doesn't mind that. He listens very carefully to me and if I suddenly shout, "Slow down!" he *does* slow down, straight away, and I can see him pulling the brakes on with his hands that are right next to my hands holding on to the handle bars.

While I'm on Daddy's bike I do a lot of feeling. I feel happy, like when we sing, but also I feel what it's like to have Daddy so close without having any fuss of giving me a cuddle or anything, and I like that. I feel all the tingly feelings of feeling him breathing so close to me, and I very nearly feel his heart, especially when it's pounding on the steep hills. And whenever I can feel that, I know that means that I'm very close to him. Another thing I feel is the nice pink cushion that he's made the most comfortable he possibly can.

So that is why I like that cushion.

The reason I'm remembering about that cushion is that I feel I need it now. I need it for sitting on, 'cos even though Uncle George's car seat is made of leather, which is supposed to be very comfortable, I'm feeling sore right in the place where I'm sitting. I wish I had Daddy's cushion to try to help it.

My mouth is making sort of twitching movements at the side, which I'm trying to stop 'cos this is the kind of twitching that happens just before you cry. I mustn't cry 'cos I mustn't let Uncle George see, in case he asks what's wrong. I simply couldn't say anything at all about what's wrong.

I'll suck my finger very hard and sort of press down on that 'cos I think that's what soldiers used to do in the war. Mum keeps telling us about her uncle who had to have a bullet taken out of him and she says he was really brave. She says we should be very grateful that things are better nowadays. Because in the olden days it was before proper anaesthetics so the doctor would give the soldiers something to bite on and he'd tell them to "press down with your teeth on this", just before he cut them open. If biting something helped the soldiers to not feel the pain of getting cut open, then I think it might help me now. So I'll use my

GOODBYE PINK ROOM

finger to help me to not feel that anything's sore in a place that I couldn't tell anyone about.

I've got my sucking-finger in my mouth and I'm pressing down on it with my teeth, and the olden-days doctors must have been right 'cos biting this is helping me not to cry now, which is a good thing.

I can't think what else I can do except to bite my finger. I don't want to say anything or especially not to cry 'cos I'd hate for Uncle George to think that I'm complaining.

What's very, very bad is that Uncle George might tell, even though I hated this, and he might say that I made it happen. That's because…

… It's because…

I'm sucking very hard on my finger.

I was already very, very frightened about the game thing that he had just been doing, and I didn't like that at all, and I was so afraid that I might be sick because…

… because of what I'd had to swallow. And I started the horrible kind of coughing that happens when you're going to be sick, and I bent over in case I might be sick, and I was a tiny bit sick and I felt as if it was my heart that I was being sick on, 'cos everything had all been so horrible.

Anyway I was bending over like that, retching, when…

… That's when he came up behind me and did the terrible thing… the really terrible thing.

And I can't remember all about it 'cos it was so dreadful but I can remember him saying I was "offering" myself and "asking for it" and wasn't I a mischief?

What did he *mean*?

What *did* he mean? When I couldn't even talk?

If only I knew, then I could make sure I never ask again.

This car seat feels very hard and not having Daddy's cushion to help the hardness is what's making me nearly cry. That's why

I just can't help wishing that I could have it here, to help me in Uncle George's car. If only I had softness or gentleness, that would help so much. Daddy's cushion from his bike.

I mustn't cry but my lips are very trembly.

I don't think that my life will ever be the same now. It can't be. Not after today.

22

Being Driven Back

I'm on the back seat of the car and I've sort of half lain down with the top half of me curled up. I'm looking at the darkness of my own shadow, here, where my face meets the leather seat-back. This way I can't see anything other than the very dark maroonness which looks lighter than this when I'm not so close to it. But at this moment it looks dark, very dark, and I quite like it seeming to be darker 'cos it's a bit mysterious and anyway I don't want to look at anything else in this world apart from this darkness.

I've stuffed my nose right up to the stitching down one of the many lines that run all the way down the seat-back like straight-line waterfalls. There's a valley in the leather where the stitching runs down and, on either side, the leather puffs out in a nice round curve that's smooth against my nose and forehead. If I breathe in deeply I can smell the smell of the leather and I like that. But I'm not going to sniff up too deeply 'cos I don't want to cause anything in my body to move. I want to keep still; keep very, very still.

Some of my hair has come out of my plaits and it's fallen over my eyes in a way that feels horrible and messy, and maybe it didn't fall properly, on its own; maybe I just told a sort of nearly-lie just then 'cos maybe I made sure my hair fell so that he wouldn't see my face. I don't want him to see me. I don't want him to be able to turn round and have a look at me and feel happy. He might get a smile inside himself if he thought I was sleeping peacefully or something, and I'm *not peaceful*. But now I think about it, it might be quite nice for him to think something and for him to be sure he's right and in fact he'd be wrong and only I would know that. Yes, I would like that. But that's not a good enough reason for me to move my hair now, 'cos I need it there. I need it, to cover me. I want to feel what it's like to feel a bit covered again. Feel it; feel it. Make myself believe it. It's all right now; everything's all right. I'll be all right; it'll all get better; I'll get better. I just need to feel what "covered up" means and believe it and feel it and that'll make everything be all right.

But it's not all right.

Don't think about that, Rose. You mustn't. You must find something else to think about…

What else can I find to think about? It must be something different; something nice and soothing. Maybe I could look out of the window? No, I don't want to 'cos I don't want to sit up. I don't want to stop feeling covered up and I don't want to stop sniffing this leather. And anyway I don't want to have to look at anything – not anything at all – in case it might be different from what I know. I can't take in anything more. Not now. Not today.

Shall I become able to think about new things again? Shall I? At school on Monday, shall I be able to think about "new" things and "different" things then? Shall I be able to listen well, and learn – like I used to – and concentrate properly? Or shall I sit down at my desk and find that my mind keeps sliding back to being here in the car, here where I feel as if I've found a little bit of rest and it's better than it was… there. I can't think about anything at all that was "there". My mind still feels as if it's going to burst and I'm concentrating very hard on not letting it.

I don't know how I'm going to keep doing this and I mustn't think about that in case that stops me concentrating and that might let my whole mind burst. I might just about manage to hold on to it, as long as I can stop it from thinking about anything else.

· ·

The trouble is, my mind can't take in anything else, at all; not even nice green fields, if we haven't finished driving past the fields. I hope we haven't. I hope we're not as far as villages or towns – oh dear, that would be much worse 'cos if we've reached towns then that means we're nearly home and I'm not ready to get to our house yet and smile hello to Mum and smile goodbye to Uncle George and say thank you for a lovely time.

The car is making its droning noise that squeaks sometimes, a bit like the hum of the wireless when it's not tuned properly and it's squealing. Maybe if I make a humming noise like the car I won't be able to hear the thoughts that I don't want to hear and that I'm trying not to, so my brain doesn't burst. I'm going to hum now in order to help that to happen. I'm going to keep my hum on the same note as the car all the time so Uncle George won't be able to hear what I'm doing. I'll be doing something else that he doesn't know and then that will be very good, because he thinks he knows all about me and this'll prove to me that he doesn't.

I don't want to sit up and I don't know how I'm going to when it's time to 'cos I just want to hide and hide and hum the car note so I can't hear anything; not anything.

How soon will we be back? He said I could lie down on the back seat and there'd be "plenty of time", but last time when he said that, the next thing was he suddenly said, "We're there now," and that was too soon – it was *too soon*, and too quick, and I hadn't finished stopping my mind from bursting. And I had to cope, which was terrible, but I'm not going to remember that 'cos I'm not going to remember anything terrible 'cos I'm trying to make my mind be all right.

It doesn't feel all right but I'm trying to make it be all right.

He said that it was all right; he said everything would be all right. But I know he's wrong. It's not all right.

I'm not going to notice that we are passing lamp-posts now and lamp-posts only happen in towns and I'm only going to

• •

notice what happens when they switch on and I'm going to make my brain think about how they start off red and then they gradually become orange and they change the colour of the dark-maroon leather. I'm watching that and I'm concentrating on colours and change. You can never tell when it's changing, you only ever notice when a new light comes on and you notice that it's more red than the last one that was orange. That must mean that you'd got used to the red turning orange without you noticing it.

That's one of the things about life. Things happen that you think are all the same, always the same going on and on, and you don't notice that something has changed, even when you were trying and trying to notice if it was changing and you didn't 'cos you couldn't 'cos it happened too gradually. I think Mum would say, "That's what you call a subtle change, Rose."

Not all changes are subtle. Some things happen very suddenly that you do notice, and you can sometimes get quite a shock. You don't know what to do but these lamp-posts turning orange are subtle and slow and I'm watching them.

If the lamp-posts are coming on, that means it must be getting dark. If it's getting dark, that must mean that it's getting to be later and we might have some supper. I feel a bit sick and Uncle George would say that's because I'm lying down in the car and I should sit up, but that's not why I feel sick.

I'm feeling sick because of other things. Because of the Happenings… things that I'm not going to think about but which I keep almost-remembering by mistake, after I'd been deliberately forgetting.

When I think about sitting up, I feel a bit as if I might cry. Oh dear, that would make me be very silly 'cos there's no reason to cry.

I don't want to be a cry-baby so I mustn't let myself think about why I might cry. So I'd better not think about trying to sit up… except, I've *got* to sit up before we get home 'cos I mustn't

– mustn't! – let him "help" me. I don't want him to touch me or come near me at all or even to look as if he cares about me.

Because of earlier.

…

…

Suddenly he's turning the corner that I recognize; he's turning into our road. Oh, quick; I've got to be right, I've got to look all right, I've got to say hello to Mum, I've got to smile, smile with my eyes not just my mouth – didn't I know what a proper smile was? Say thank you to Uncle George! Thank you for a lovely time; come along…

23

Something Must've Happened

It's Sunday evening and I wish I didn't have to come home early like this, but I did have to.

And I mustn't let that tear in my eye fall down my cheek – not while I'm right in the middle of this bus and the lady over there might see me – and anyway I shouldn't cry at all. I don't want to be a cry-baby. So I must stop myself from being silly.

Oh dear: I wonder if it's selfish for me to have spent the money on this bus instead of putting it into the collection plate at church? I've spent money on myself instead of giving it to God. Oh dear, I really don't mean to be selfish. Oh; oh…

I mustn't panic. No. I won't panic. Because there is the *fact* that God understands us, so He must know that I didn't aim to be selfish. And I did have to come out of church. I had to. Because I was getting worse until I felt unable to think of anything other than to imagine how nice it would be to lie down. I wish I could be at home straight away instead of having to finish this journey.

On the other hand, I'm so frightened of what they'll say when I get home, and I don't know how I'll answer their questions, and I wish there could be nobody there 'cos then nobody would ever ask me anything.

I don't know what Mum's going to say, or Dad, when I arrive back early from church. I wish they could be out when I do get home but I'm pretty sure they won't be. I hope my brothers will be out 'cos otherwise they'll hear all about it – me – and I don't want them to and I don't want to talk and I don't want to get asked questions and I'm sure I will be and I don't know how I'm going to face everything.

I don't want Mum to get her serious face on but I fear she will. I know it's all because she cares about me, and the trouble is that she thinks I reject her. But that's not true at all. It's just that I don't know what to do to stop her having such a serious face, and I can't cope with all the questions. Or she might say that if I needed to leave church, then there must be something seriously wrong with me and we'd better get Dr Nathan… and that mustn't happen. But Mum might rush ahead and phone him, which would make everything get terribly tangled. Nobody will understand what's wrong 'cos the whole trouble is that I don't know myself. At least, I don't know properly. All I know is that this feels like something I've felt before sometime, but I don't know when. I think it's best for us to leave everything alone, and for no one to look or think or ask anything. Just hope that it gets better.

Oh, I wish this wasn't happening.

If Mum does get all serious it might be like that other Sunday when this happened and I went and lay down on my bed and she came in when I wasn't expecting her to. I think she had been sorting out the washing in the airing cupboard and, seeing as it's right next to my bedroom, it only took a few steps for her to come into my room. That's how she found me when I wasn't expecting her to come in. But of course as soon as she saw me lying down, she sort of gasped as if I must have had something really serious wrong with me. She asked me what was wrong and her face looked a bit cross. I started crying – well, just tears spilling – but that was enough for her to go off to find Dad and bring him to my room to help (she said). They both stood there looking, asking me what was wrong and, when I couldn't answer well enough 'cos I didn't know and I just couldn't explain, Dad said maybe it was something to do with the "women's things" so we'd better leave it at that.

Although it was a great relief that he made the questioning stop, I wished he hadn't said that 'cos I felt embarrassed. I mean, him saying it made it suddenly all public, and I am shy. I think Dad was a bit shy too, probably.

I don't want any questioning to happen again when I get home today but I don't know how I can stop it.

I really want to be private. I hate when I'm not allowed to be private. Mum says I'm secretive, but I think secret is different from private.

Mum gets so worried, which is something I wish she didn't keep doing.

Also, another trouble is that I'm a bit worried that something is very sore sort of deep inside my tummy. It feels uncomfortable, and as if something's wrong, all the way round very low down in my tummy; right down to where I'm sitting.

What I'm most frightened about is why it feels so sore there. The trouble is that if I think about it – which I just did then, accidentally – I feel as if I'm being reminded of something. Just something vague. And I cannot bear to think about that, 'cos I feel such a rush of dread and fear.

This is awful. I'll simply have to stop myself from thinking about it…

It's just that I don't know what's wrong. I hope there's nothing serious happening. I just want to curl up around myself and be left alone.

I wish I could understand what *is* happening, but I just don't. I don't know and I can't think. My brain has flooded since a minute ago; completely flooded so I can't be logical at all. That began to happen while I left church, which is why I didn't know what to say when Susan's dad followed me out and he called to me. Oh, that was so awful; so embarrassing! I thought I was safe; I thought I'd crept out without being seen. I'd waited until everyone else had stood up to shake hands with one another (the proper name is "Giving the Peace") and when they were all milling around, I'd slipped out and walked away so quietly…

How did Susan's dad notice me? I don't know. But there I was, just beginning to relax from the fact that I *had* got out of church and I was just beginning to walk to the main road when his voice boomed out from behind me, calling, "Rose?" (He's got a very deep voice; it's very low and I think he makes it sound even lower because he holds his chin down and some men do that.)

And again, as if he wasn't just calling me but he was telling me to stop: "Rose!"

I nearly turned round to him, but then I told myself that if I didn't turn round he would believe that I hadn't heard him, so I kept walking away from the church door and towards the bus stop. But the next thing was that I heard footsteps behind me, and they were walking so fast that they were almost running; and then I heard my name a third time, more urgently this time. "Rose! Rose! Are you all right?"

So I had to turn round then – it would have been very discourteous of me not to – and that was when I saw for definite that it was Susan's father, and I felt most terribly shy. That's why I answered him so quickly, like a reflex: "Yes, yes, I'm fine." I tried to give the kind of smile that would make him believe me and stop looking at me, but I could see the doubt in his face. (He was right, because I wasn't "fine" at all.) He sort of tilted his head to one side and, now that I think back and remember about it, I'd say that he had a face that was very kind. Yes, the kindness was gentle and sincere and it's too late now but I wish I could have trusted him. But I couldn't. I just couldn't trust, and I couldn't *possibly* have let myself get into a car on my own with another man.

I felt so silly and incredibly awkward.

At that moment, our eyes met and he said, "Rose, I don't want to intrude…" (or if I haven't got the exact words, it was something like that), "but perhaps you're not very well?" What made the deepest impression was that, when he said that, he didn't seem to be invading me, and he didn't come closer or touch me or put his arm round me like…

… Oops, no. I mustn't let my mind remember anything like that…

… He didn't force me to tell him what was wrong. He didn't ask me any questions at all. That was a relief, 'cos I didn't know any answers. He stayed very gentle towards me, and he tilted his head again as if he was checking that I really, really was all right.

I expect he must have seen that I wasn't, but I couldn't bear to be near to anyone. So we stood there outside church, and I was trying to edge myself away – I was desperate to be on my own – and Susan's father said, "Honestly, Rose. Won't you *please* let me give you a lift home?" His voice was so gentle, and his whole manner was so respectful towards me, that I found tears welling up before I could stop them, which suddenly felt so shameful that I simply *had* to find a way of escaping as quickly as I could. I couldn't possibly have accepted his offer. Not possibly!

The situation got more and more embarrassing 'cos there was something in his manner that allowed me to believe that there was truly no trick. All he wanted was to be supportive 'cos he had seen that I was in need. But I didn't know how to receive his sincerity…

I could tell that he didn't want me to feel uncomfortable with him. That must be why he started to walk away slowly, backwards, even though I think he knew that I wasn't fine. But he showed respect to me, and he let me say no. I must have looked very silly for rejecting him.

I'm very sore in a deep down place that I can't mention and daren't think about.

What am I going to *do* when I get home?

Don't think about that, Rose. Check where we've got to…

It's all right. It's not time to get off yet.

• •

SOMETHING MUST'VE HAPPENED   181

… I'm dreading the fuss I'll meet when I get home. If they ask me any questions at all, that'll feel like a fuss. The only thing I want is to be allowed to go to my room all on my own and lie down. I don't want any questions from anyone…

Actually, that's not absolutely all I want. I would like a hot water bottle as well. I would like something warm and soothing on my tummy, 'cos that's like the centre of where everything's gone wrong. And I'd also like for Mum to be in a nice, kind mood…

The trouble is I can't risk Mum being cross and I can't quite work out whether or not she would be if I said something. I don't think she should be. Except she might, because she might tell me I've done something wrong, which maybe I did, a long time ago, but I just don't know how to cope with all that, which is why I can't contemplate it.

Oh, I wish I could test to see if she *would* be cross if I told her some bits, because she isn't always cross. Sometimes when she comes to kiss me goodnight she's all warm and gentle, and other times when she giggles I think I should trust her more. I feel I'm a bad daughter for not trusting her to be like that all the time.

But on a Sunday evening she's likely to be busy and distracted, because she's got everything to sort out ready for the new week beginning tomorrow.

Everything has all got too complicated… If I told her anything about my sore tummy, she might ask more and more, and she might find out more than I could bear. How can I expect her to understand, when I'm mixed up about it all myself?

I must make myself be more grown up. I'm sitting here on this bus, feeling as frightened as if I were a child! I'm a teenager!

I'm still wishing Mum could be in a soft, gentle mood, and it's possible that she might be – except you never know beforehand. Sometimes you think she'll be okay and then if you ask her something that you think is just telling the truth, suddenly you find that it's the wrong thing 'cos she'll suddenly be very cross.

GOODBYE PINK ROOM

Then you find that she's been "hard pressed" at school, or the finances aren't working out, or something, and you wish you hadn't asked for help at all, but you don't know how to be kind to her either. So you just go away and hide in case you do something else that you find out later is wrong.

Sometimes I think to myself that when I want to talk to Mum about something, it would be better if I could "Apply". Because if I was allowed to say, "May I apply for your loving attention?" then my request would be like an application form that was sitting on her desk at work, and when she *did* have time she'd be able to deal with it. She would either be like she is when she comes to kiss me goodnight, or else she could just say, "No" or "Not at the moment, dear. Later."

Oh dear, I'm nearly crying again. You mustn't cry on a bus. I must keep my face turned so I'm looking out of the window in case somebody notices what my face looks like. The fact is, I've got no reason to cry! Why would I cry? Rose, are you listening to me? There is no reason to cry! Stop being silly!

What's wrong? I don't know. I can't tell. All I know is that I want to go home and curl up around a hot water bottle. (There, I managed to be more grown up and I didn't say the silly phrase of having a "hottie on my tummy".)

The bus is nearly at the end of Bridge Road now, where the bus stops and it's not far for me to walk home.

Oh dear. I want to be home but I also don't want to be.

I'm praying inside myself now but dear Jesus, I don't know what words to say. I'm just thinking of You and hoping that You'll make my thoughts into a prayer because You understand, don't You? I can't explain anything, and I don't know what are the right words, and I don't know what to say…

Oh, I do wish this weren't happening. What *is* happening?

I wish I could work things out.

· ·

24

Getting Dressed

I'm in the middle of getting dressed for school but I've stopped and I'm not quite sure why, especially 'cos I always get dressed very quickly so my brothers don't say I'm a slow-coach and girls always take longer to dress than boys.

I'm not a slow-coach and they shouldn't tell me I am, and I always try to race them.

But that's why I'm confused as to why I've stopped and why I'm just standing here in my room now, in the middle of getting dressed. Here I am with my tie round my neck and I'm not tying it. At least, I've started to and I've made the knot, but when I got up to the bit where you have to pull the knot up to your neck, I stopped. I didn't want to pull it up.

It was as if I couldn't.

It was as if, if I did that, I would cause myself to feel that my tie was going to go round my neck like hands going round my neck, and as if my tie might strangle me. As if everything suddenly got violent – more violent than I've ever seen in all my life. Eyes grown big, and bulging, and suddenly terror. Red alert. Emergency. Can't breathe. Paralysis. Look at his eyes… He's furious with me. *He's trying to strangle me!*

No, no, no! That can only be my imagination. Silly imagination!

I'm still standing here, as if I've been caught in a trap and I can't move.

I'm just staring in front of me, and staring and staring, and I can't think properly and I don't know why.

What am I doing?

I don't know. I feel as if I'm in a sort of daze. I hate it and I hate myself 'cos I must be stupid 'cos just look at me.

If I don't hurry up now, I'll be late for breakfast and when I get downstairs they'll say I'm slow. So I mustn't be slow and I want to hurry up and I know I must and that's why I wish I could understand why I'm not getting on 'cos I do know I've got to.

Hurry up, Rose!

But I can't.

I'm stuck.

But I'm chanting the Rule that I have which says I'm never allowed to think about Uncle George's outings. Not ever again. That's all in the past, and I've got to not think about the past. The present is what's important. I'm allowed to think about the present, and I'm allowed to try to understand that, but I mustn't think about the past 'cos the past is behind me. Everyone says that, especially people who were in the war like Granddad, and they say that's how to survive, so that means it's all right for me to say the same as they do. The past is behind me. Don't dwell on the past. Don't think about the past, Rose. Everything that's not nice has been put in your pretend-cupboard, and the door is shut, and that's Final.

That's all very well but I wish I knew what was happening now – in the present – 'cos I feel very, very stupid that I don't understand why I should get stuck in the middle of getting dressed.

It's just that I can't make my tie be tight.

I can't seem to bear the thought of anything around my neck.

I can't bear the feeling of something getting tighter and tighter till it's so tight that I maybe won't be able to breathe properly.

But that isn't happening. Not now. Snap out of it, Rose! And hurry up!

Right. I'm going to hurry up. I'm getting ready to pull my

tie up. I'm taking a big breath in. And when I pull, I'm going to make sure I do it in one smooth movement that's not a sudden jerk but nice, and gentle, and that'll make it be all right. I'm holding the knot ready in my right hand now, and I'm holding the short piece in my left hand. And I'm going to pull so I drag the knot to the top.

Dad calls the short piece the "tail". But I mustn't think about Dad even if I want to because it's no use, because he's gone to work now. I heard him leave the house earlier and I wanted to go downstairs to give him a kiss goodbye – he always likes when I do that – but this morning I didn't because, when I heard him in the kitchen beneath my room while I lay in bed, I was thinking about lots of things. I'm not going to remember what I was thinking 'cos that would be looking backwards and I mustn't look back. You don't get on in life if you look back.

I must get on in my life. I must look forwards.

I must finish getting dressed.

Come on, Rose. Hurry up. Hurry up.

I'm standing here on this one spot telling myself what to do but I haven't done it. I haven't moved. I must look as if I've been frozen till I'm like a statue. Actually, I know what the word is: it's petrified. From the Greek, *petros*, which means stone. Miss Flowers told us that because she knows Greek as well as Latin. She said it was good to understand the words we use, and I've just remembered how she told us all that being "petrified" meant being like a stone statue.

I must look like a stone statue now and that's 'cos I'm feeling frightened about something and I haven't worked out exactly what it is.

There can only be one reason for me being petrified and thinking such nonsense and the reason is this: I must be stupid.

But I'm not stupid. Something here doesn't make sense, and I simply want to understand what's wrong.

No. I must force myself to hurry up, otherwise I'll become a slow-coach as well and the boys could chant at me being a stupid girly slow-coach. I don't think I have got anywhere left inside myself to bear anything else, like hearing mocking... Please, please, I wish I didn't have to get mocked, even though Mum says it's all just fun and you've got to take the rough and tumble of life.

I mustn't cry. Oh, Rose, don't cry!

I just felt myself give a big swallow, and I felt myself lift my throat upwards when I swallowed so that I could make space for what I was swallowing to go down.

A wail crept up on me as I did that – a howl, a cry, a scream. Oh, this is so terrible! Some days, life seems really terrible, and I don't know how to do it. I'm all alone, and I can't tell anyone, or ask about things, and oh God, why can't I just come to heaven to be with You?

I'm putting my head in my hands. I'm trying to hold my brain straight, so I can work out how to live.

I've got to snap out of this. I've got to hurry up.

What can I do? I still feel so dazed and stunned and afraid and nearly crying.

I know. If I go over to my dressing table and look into the mirror, then instead of thinking about something getting tight round my neck, what I'll do is I'll concentrate on watching my tie in the reflection.

That'll help.

Here I am. I can see the black and white stripes of my tie now. I like the pattern of the stripes, and the way the white stripes are thin and narrow and they come after a thick stripe of black. I like my school uniform. I feel smart. I like that.

Someone else says things about how I look and I almost thought about him but very quickly I stopped myself – just in time – 'cos the cupboard door is shut and I am not going to think anything at all about him or about his compliments.

Look in the mirror, Rose. Look at your tie. Get ready, 'cos I'm about to pull the tie up and you can concentrate on how your collar looks once you've pulled your tie straight.

I'm closing my eyes, and I'm starting now, and I'm pulling my tie up. One nice, smooth, gentle movement, and listen – Rose, stop your mind from wandering! – listen to the slight swishing noise as the material of the knot swishes up the tail and it's going towards the top button of my shirt. And now open your eyes and, quick, think about your collar, Rose. Don't think about your neck, or what he… or anything.

That's right, just pull your white collar down and over the tie and see! You look nice. Your tie is tied and your collar is down over it, hiding the tight bit, and your whole shirt looks nice and you look nice.

That's that bit done. Now, quick, you've taken a long time so far, all because of something you were being stupid about. You'll have to make up for the lost time by being extra-speedy pulling on your skirt and cardigan that Granny knitted, then socks – nice clean white ones for Monday morning – and shoes that Dad polished, which he does every Sunday evening, and then brush your hair…

… and now you're ready. At last. You're ready.

Look in the mirror again and smile. Good.

Ready to go downstairs.

Keep the cupboard door closed. Remember the Rule. Don't think about anything that's happened, and is finished now. Finished!

If I'm quick, I think I'll still get down before my brothers and that'll make things be a bit better.

Please God, help today to be a good day and help me to concentrate very well in school.

Quick!

. . . .

GETTING DRESSED

25

Look to the Future

The sun is warm on my cheeks and I'm enjoying that sensation so much that I've turned my whole face to receive all that this summer sunshine might give me.

It's lunch-break. I'm lying here on the grass of the school playing field, and the four of us friends are all lying in a row: Ruth, Susan, Mary, and me. Mostly we're quiet, not talking, simply enjoying ourselves and one another because we are all good friends.

I have no idea what any of the others are thinking but there's something rather nice about how we're all here together and yet we're also each being separate. I wonder what Ruth's thinking about now?… or Mary? or Susan? Are their minds scanning what they did in lessons this morning? Or what they'll be doing this afternoon? We all do different subjects now that we're in the sixth form, so we've been split up from being in the same classes. Are they planning their homework, or maybe they're thinking about what happens at home, or their parents or their family or Youth Group or… anything!

It's strange that we can all be lying so close to one another yet we have no idea of what's going on inside each other's brains, even though physically – geographically! – our heads are so close together. Our thoughts will be miles apart from one another; each of us totally self-contained and separate. Brains and minds are extraordinary things: so intricate, so clever, so private.

I'm private. No one knows what I'm thinking. Not one of these friends knows what's going on inside me now: in fact, they don't know anything about lots of things, and sometimes I wish they did but it's too late now. It's all over and past now with Uncle George and it'll never happen again. I don't go down that road any more. It's fine. I'm fine. All's well that ends well.

Don't even remember that, Rose.

I need to be careful that I don't relax completely, 'cos I can find, occasionally, that my thoughts have accidentally gone sliding down the chute that still seems to exist in my mind. It's been so for some while now… for how long, I wonder? Anyway, I know I must work hard at steering clear of that happening and I do. As long as I catch myself in time, I'll push the negative thoughts, the silly thoughts, away.

The trouble is, of course, I'm sometimes caught unawares and find I'm suddenly feeling terrible. Terrible and afraid and lost and childish. Silly me! How ridiculous!

Which is, of course, one reason why I need to keep myself private. I don't want to show up how silly I am underneath.

Anyway, I'm alert at this moment and I'm consciously looking upwards. In fact, I'm not only looking upwards in my mind, but also (*non solum… sed etiam!*) I'm looking upwards even physically. I can feel now that my whole head is looking upwards – up, towards the sun – and I've raised my chin away from my chest a little more than usual such that, even though my eyes are closed, I'm looking up. *I am looking up*.

That's very important.

I'm glad to have Ruth, Susan, and Mary as friends. I enjoy their company – we enjoy one another – and although normally we're chatting together all the time, occasionally, like now, we will just "be", lying together side by side. We feel very close and we don't have to talk.

But here we are, all lying in a row, relaxing together. We've got about ten minutes before the bell will ring. We all decided in the refectory that today was a day when it would be nice to walk across to the playing field for as much of our lunch-break as possible, so we all ate quickly enough to make it worthwhile to get here and flop on the grass before we're due back in class. Flop: just flop. That's all we're doing. Lying here lazily, enjoying, letting the sun beam down on us and invigorate us ready for this afternoon. Next year we won't be able to be so lazy 'cos we'll have to be on duty as prefects. Each of us has been chosen to be a prefect: except Ruth who's going to be Head Girl.

I love just lying here doing nothing except plucking at the blades of grass occasionally and letting them drop lazily through my fingers. I love the smell of the grass. And I love the sound of the birdsong.

When I was on my own – when I used to lie in the grass with – with – I mustn't say, mustn't think – but just to finish that thought, I used not to hear the birds. I wonder why I didn't. Did they not sing? Did they know that something was going wrong; something was happening that was serious – terribly serious – and this was nothing to sing about? Or were there no birds? Perhaps there were no birds 'cos there were no bushes where we went the last few trips out. He drove me so far onto the moors, it seemed we went further away from where bushes grew. He took me so far away. We were all alone. There was no one to call to, to shout to, to scream to. In any case, I couldn't have screamed. The only sound was of the breeze as it blew across the moor. He didn't speak and I didn't speak. He just did what he did, and I let him. I let him. Why did I let him?…

Aaagh! Quick! Shut that cupboard door! Stop it, Rose! Stop it immediately!

How did you get there? How did you start thinking about that? You weren't supposed to look down!

It's fine; everything is fine. This is a lovely lunch-hour and nothing like that is happening. It probably never happened. Good gracious, what were you thinking just then? You are here, Rose. You're lying with your friends, relaxing.

It might help to open my eyes, and then I might manage to not think.

I can see clouds scudding across the sky.

"Scudding". That's a nice word. I shall think about scudding so that I keep steering my thoughts away from the chute.

Does a poet use that word? Isn't there a poem somewhere that talks about "scudding"?

I don't know.

I can't think.

I wish I could think properly.

Look up, Rose. Don't look down. Keep looking up.

… What was I thinking when I lost my train of thought?

Oh yes, I was thinking about becoming prefects and how this must be the last term when we can doodle like this because we don't have duties. That's right.

Look up, Rose. Keep looking up.

What's ahead? What's coming up? Exams soon! But the good news is that although the exams are coming up soon, they're not as bad as last year's, and we don't have to revise all lunchtime because we have study periods now we're in the sixth form. Anyway we four have all agreed to give ourselves time off revision this lunchtime, which is why we're all lying relaxing here, and it's very nice.

Oh, I hope I'll be able to concentrate on my revision. I must… I just *must!* If I don't, what will Mum say? What if I don't do well enough in my exams?

You've got to, Rose.

What will I do whenever I get lost, and I can't think?

Count your blessings: that's it. Count your blessings and all will be well.

I'm looking upwards, and the sun is beating down on me. I like thinking of the way some poets describe how the sun "kisses one's cheeks". That's a nice thought and I'm trying to imagine that my cheeks are being kissed by the sun.

The sun is so gentle. It doesn't have a nasty smell. It doesn't come too close; in fact, it never comes closer. It always stays where it is. The sun's kisses are safe, and gentle, and nice.

I feel safe. I feel safe with the sun kissing me and I feel safe 'cos my friends are beside me. We're all lying in a row, all relaxing after lunch and before our afternoon classes.

I'm looking forward, and up; as Granny said, "Forget about the past and look to the future." I shall continue to do so, no matter what. In fact, I'm going to keep my eyes open, because that will probably help.

The younger girls from the other year groups are mostly standing or running or playing games, rather than lying lazily as we are. They're running free.

Am I free?

I hope so.

I'm trying to be.

I'll just drink in the last few minutes of laziness and companionship and niceness lying in this grass.

I'll lie here and count my blessings. And I'll pray. God, help me. Please. Make me forget. Blot it out. Let it be as if it never was. Like You do with our sins: just remove them "as far as the east is from the west", as the Bible says. Please, God.

Please.

26

Compost-Making

I thought it would all rot, and I knew what "rot" meant because when I was very little I used to help our gardener-man to make piles of compost that he showed me gradually rotting. He would take my hand and take me to look afresh at the big pile we'd made together some months before; and he'd show me how it had disintegrated. Bend down, he'd say, and peep in. Look deep down. Excitedly I'd stoop down and look very closely and, sure enough, "our" green leaves and stalks and orange carrot peelings would have lost their shapes and turned dark in colour; and sometimes things at the bottom of the pile would even go into liquid that oozed and squelched if I poked at it. Time did that, said the gardener-man to me: time and the darkness. It was a little secret for me to learn for when I was a big girl.

I was a big girl now, in the sixth form. Since I knew what rotting meant, and since time and darkness were the essential ingredients, I expected that whatever I pushed into the cupboard of my mind would rot, just like our compost. It had darkness and with time too it would go away. Disintegrate. Turn to liquid that would seep down into the earth until there would be nothing to be seen of it at all.

Many people say, "Time heals."

Passage of Time (3)

Several decades
Daddy dies
Career; marriage; infertility; foster-children
Trying, always, to appear normal
Uncle George dies

27

Facing the Demons

But my experiences were not vegetation and they didn't rot. They lay untouched, unlooked at. Oh, they had time all right – decades – and darkness too, because I didn't allow myself to think about them. But they weren't of the right material to turn into nothing. History remains solid. What happened didn't go away. No matter what I told myself, the facts remained. They didn't change. And they refused to do so, which frightened me.

I hadn't got rid of any of it. Couldn't. I had endured, not explored. The pressure of all that lay inside my cupboard actually increased instead of decreasing, in spite of all I was doing to hold the door shut. I had to work harder to maintain my denial. News reports of children being interfered with stirred up an inordinate distress in me. Although I tried to remain detached, as if such reports had nothing to do with me, I knew deep down that they were touching a deep chord. I grabbed for excuses to cover my inner responses, desperate to minimize my experiences, repeating to myself, "But nothing much happened to me."

With hindsight, I see that there had been a tiny shift from my saying, "Nothing happened…" to "Nothing much happened." That little chink proved to be profoundly significant. Like a wedge, it prevented me from being able to close the door completely. In time, the pressure of all that lay behind it broke through. The story that I could not tolerate hearing began to tell itself.

Then I met someone whom I can only describe as having been sent by God. Our meeting must have been at the "right" time, when I was ready to shed the weight of carrying everything alone and she, recognizing the signs of abuse, received me in a different way. Gradually, gradually, she won my trust. She must surely have been sent by God. How could I have trusted again? Yet I did trust her. I trusted her experience of life and her love of God. However, even with God as our guide, the journey proved more difficult than I would ever have imagined. God does not give us protection from our humanity. I recall saying quite frequently, when things became difficult, "There is only one Saviour, and that is not you!"

I was perplexed by some of my bizarre reactions, and I was weary of trying to cover them. I could see that I was being tetchy and hypersensitive despite all my best efforts to look normal. With the comfort of her listening, I began to talk, just hinting obliquely at first. I maybe imagined that this nice person listening would have a black sack to receive all the things from my cupboard without my having to look at them all properly myself, and that I would be relieved. After all, the theory is that a problem shared is a problem halved.

The person whom God had sent drew close enough to stay with me on those occasions when I was caught off balance. She was kind when she saw me struggling, trying, trying so desperately to maintain the denial and cover my distress. And when she saw me like that, she didn't dismiss me as crazy. She seemed to be able to accept me with my distress and my confusion, even while I was busy dismissing any possibility of "something" being wrong. "It's nothing!" I kept insisting, persuading myself, but I saw that she remained unconvinced. Yet I also saw that steady compassion in her eyes. I saw questions to which I did not know the answers and I wanted to understand myself. Anyway, having been alone with the problem all these years, I felt a relief as I experienced an understanding that I had never dreamed to be possible.

. . . .

GOODBYE PINK ROOM

I think that the gentleness I experienced in her response to me was enough to give me the courage to lift the latch on the door of my cupboard. I began to voice my questions. What was happening when I was being tetchy? Why was I overreacting? From what was I defending myself so vehemently?

I feared she wouldn't believe what would come out if I put words to what lay in the mist of my mind. I myself hadn't believed it for almost thirty-five years. Why should anyone else?

It was better unbelieved, anyway.

Except, something was changing. Again, I can only say that God Himself must have been my guide. How else could I have been turned around from my strong resolve never to look back?

Whenever she seemed to understand, I began to say a little more about myself. I was nervous when I said anything "significant". How would she react? I would watch her face with enormous apprehension. I tried not to let my watching be seen, but I was alert to every slightest twitch in her expression, every movement of her mouth, every flicker of an eyebrow, every sign that would prove what I was so certain to be true... namely that she wouldn't be able to stay patient while I struggled to find words for the truth. I didn't think I could bear to hear it myself. One promise from the lips of Jesus took on a particular significance, and that promise acted like a beacon to keep me going: "The truth will set you free."[3] I was treading a fine line between my conviction that the truth would be the key to real freedom, and my fear that I myself would find my own story quite unbearable. I thought it made me a horrible slut.

But she didn't treat me as if I was unbearable, even when I hinted at the worst things. Instead, she loved me. Sadly, that word "love" is frequently misconstrued and misinterpreted. I hesitate to use it, but love is the correct word. She loved me, no matter

---

3   John 8:32 NIV.

what I told her and no matter how I recoiled at myself. It was almost as if she were giving flesh to our belief that God loves us no matter what.

I felt real relief as I was beginning to be understood. I found compassion instead of judgment, and compassion is a hallmark of God. Hope and light began to filter into the darkest corners of my mind.

Was I wooed by the relief? Was I naïve to lift the latch of that firmly closed door? I felt warmed and comforted as I talked, but – and this "but" is so important – as my story went into words, it became more real. I was daring to face my own demons, but in doing so I became exposed to *more* pain, not less. That was not what I had expected and I became terrified. I was no longer able to deny the truth.

I now realize that all our defence mechanisms need to be treated with respect. They are like dressings over wounds; they protect us; they enable us to survive. I still have several: for example, when things get too painful I go out into the cold to numb my mind so I can return more ready to carry on with the day. Or if my mind becomes flooded with images I can't bear, I might try to distract myself or even make my mind go blank. At other times I can do a "flip", behaving as if everything is fine, telling myself that nothing has happened. Sometimes I get through by chanting instructions: "Do this, do that, do the other…"

There was some benefit in my "telling". First I felt relief, then grief. Then, as my grief was comforted each time, I was given more hope of healing. I was given substance to the faith that I had sustained ever since childhood, that God was indeed with me.

GOODBYE PINK ROOM

28

I Spun Down Again

I was out walking with my friend one day, enjoying the birdsong and flowers in beautiful countryside, when suddenly, without warning, we were both given a terrible shock.

We were chatting together and I found myself sharing with her some of what I was discovering about life in general, and I told her a few more specific things about "Uncle" George. She was listening to me gently, which must have encouraged me to open up a little bit more. She surprised me because suddenly, unexpectedly, she became angry about George. She didn't merely say that she felt angry, but she actually *was* angry and she began to beat the ground with a stick that she'd picked up beneath the tree. And (even talking about it now takes me back there) her anger was like a catalyst in a chemical experiment: it precipitated a reaction in me. Suddenly I could not speak. I simply could not speak.

I was shocked. I felt terrified. I became like a child lost in a trance-like state. I couldn't explain. I had spun down again; fallen into a void that was not denial, and it was not a trance, but a shocked state as if "everything" had just happened again. I could have been back on the moors with George getting angry, just as he had done on that terrible, terrible occasion…

I panicked, feeling at the mercy of whatever was going to happen next. I didn't know what it was but was gripped by the fear that it would be something terrible.

Neither of us knew what to do.

Somehow, from somewhere, I mustered all my strength and I forced myself to whisper two words. "Something's happened."

I thought that I had given a whole speech; that those two words revealed everything that had ever happened with George. I expected that she would have her eyes opened to all that I was seeing when I thought of the word, "happened", and that therefore she would understand everything. But of course she didn't understand. She hardly knew anything. As far as she was concerned, we were out for a lovely walk and nothing had happened at all. She had simply expressed anger on my behalf, and surely that was normal.

What was going on? She didn't know that Uncle George had ever become angry with me and neither did I, consciously – I'd blocked it all out until that moment when her anger cracked open my memory so that I found myself totally out of my depth, faced with a panorama of all the Happenings on the moor.

She was frightened and bewildered by the severity of my reaction. She told me later that I looked pale and shocked: she could see that something terrible had happened to me. Yet she had been with me all the time; we were out in beautiful countryside. Why was I rigid with fear?

She didn't know that putting me into a car and driving me home would make things even worse, but it did. My mind was full of just one thing: something had happened and I was being driven home. With every lamp-post we passed, my terror was reinforced.

Only two things ran through my mind. The first, which I managed to articulate, was "Something's happened." The second thing was a scream that I could only express with action, not words. After she'd dropped me off at the bridge as usual just before home, I stopped half-way across and just stared and stared at the river flowing so fast, far below. I stared for over an hour. I wanted to jump. But I didn't have the courage.

GOODBYE PINK ROOM

I am only just growing able to put all this terrifying tangle into words. I had been flung back into a re-run of George. That experience in the countryside had me realize (later) that my life will never, ever be the same because of what happened with George. He changed things in a drastic way. My world collapsed. It shattered. The line of my history changed course.

When Humpty Dumpty fell off his wall, all the king's horses and all the king's men couldn't put Humpty together again. Why? Because once the egg has cracked open, the white oozes out and the yolk breaks its sac, then that yolk cannot be cajoled back into its sac. The two have mixed, and the shell has shattered. No matter how many people work on it, that egg can never be whole, unblemished, unbroken.

After that day in the countryside, I realized that my defences that had previously protected me had crumbled; they no longer held as before. Everything started to tumble out, too fast – more than I could cope with. If I found it hard to hold myself together on that particular day, I found it even harder afterwards.

From that day on, I no longer had the hiding-place of the previous thirty-five years. Once out, images from the past pursued me both day and night. When I closed my eyes to seek relaxation, my mind switched wide open so that I saw what I had previously managed to avoid or dismiss. When I sought relief in sleep, I met the same scenes but distorted into nightmares. I could not get away from the images: wherever I went I was pursued by the whole, painful story. I was plagued with ghastly flashbacks, nightmares; or I would get locked into seeing re-runs of the Happenings like film shows every night.

I am still in the process of being "healed" from all this.

29

I Feel Sick

I feel terribly sick.

I often feel sick but I can't speak about it. How do I explain to you; to *anyone?* How do I explain that I am wishing I were somewhere where there are very caring people that could see me and who'd care for me as if something Very Terrible Indeed had just happened to me. They would open their arms to hold me if they saw me in the corridor; and guide me to where to sit, if I'd got stuck standing somewhere. They'd know that all of my body was crying a lament and they'd stroke it – me – in order to soothe; only they'd do that very, very carefully so as not to poke, only stroke. They'd very, very tenderly lead me to have a bath and they'd do very gentle swishing of the water. They'd be very, very careful indeed where they touched and they would show gentleness towards my neck where I'd nearly been… where he'd put his hands round there and he'd tried… you know.

But one problem is that my legs, which used to be his way In… my legs would need to feel the reassurance that they're not Blamed, and they would only know that by experiencing the caring person to be gentle. Very gentle. And my eyes would have to see the caring person's face to make sure that they were being gentle sincerely and not just doing it with their hands, like a job. I'd have to be sure that they wanted to be soothing to me because of a gentleness from inside them, not because they were doing a job out of duty and merely following instructions.

• •

I'm very silent on the outside because I can't think of anywhere where it would be possible for me to be given all that I want. I fear I must be yielding to the most terrible selfishness because I want this niceness so acutely that I feel that I don't "want" it but that in fact I "need" it. So I keep finding myself wondering if it wouldn't help if I said out loud to the world: "I can't do this on my own!"

But I can't imagine ever even whispering that, never mind shouting it out loud.

Could I ever do that? Should I? Is it creative? Would it be a sign of healing or inappropriate dependence?

The older I become, the more I learn about responsibility, and now I know that I ought to be able to *ask* for this help if I need it. That implies that it's my fault if the kind of help I get from those who love me isn't the right sort – I'm surrounded by love of both friends and family. So if I'm pining here for something that I feel I need, and if I don't ask, then they can't know how terribly gentle they need to be. They can only make judgments from what they observe. I think that if others see my need for "disproportionate" gentleness (disproportionate to the present, maybe, but not to my history), I can see how they'd judge me to be over-demanding, attention-seeking, or mad, which I reckon to be a quick way of busy people not thinking too hard. Everyone seems to be very busy in this life and they're distracted by their important busyness and work. Anyway, I know how to do a "flip" mostly, which means that I can pretend I'm fine and everything's in the toy cupboard and I can look as if there's nothing there and I'm fine.

Nobody knows what's in my head. They see my pretty dress and my smile. Nobody knows why I feel sick. I know now, although it's taken me about fourteen years to discover why. My "knowing" is peculiar, because even still I want only to forget and to move on. I did do that for nearly thirty-five years, copying how my grandparents coped with their memories of the war. I put

GOODBYE PINK ROOM

effort into pushing thoughts away, and I managed to "forget"…
except that I did keep feeling sick…

I don't actually believe that I am mad – only very badly hurt, which is different. The wound runs very deep and is hard to understand. Therefore I should not expect others to be as gentle as I want them to be. That's why I must get on with doing all the things I'm Supposed to do, which is what people call living life.

And because I'm so well practised in my "flip" into (so-called) "living life", I don't think that any of those people realize how much I need. I fear that they'd consider me to be very, very selfish if I told them. Many of us get by without talking about these things. Except, earlier today someone at home did ask, "Are you all right?" and my simple "Yes" didn't get questioned. So that was that.

That's how it should be – I think – except that, just occasionally, I fear I might not quite manage to carry off this quiet deception to its completion. And if I don't, I might have jumped off the merry-go-round of this world before I've had time to stop myself.

I feel so sick.

30

Covering

Did my words make sense just then? Did you understand? And if not, did you just skim over it with a "Never mind, let's keep going…"? Because if so, then that is exactly what I'm talking about.

You see, I was trying to speak but I wrapped what I meant to say in a soft blanket. I didn't want to burden you and I didn't want to expose myself. But did the blanket muffle my voice too much? Did it make the meaning unclear? How can I say the unspeakable without straining you?

"Just occasionally, I fear I might not quite manage to carry off this quiet deception to its completion."

I try. I try to live, and to stay living. I do understand that it's not fair for me to expect others to be as gentle as I want them to be. Therefore I get on with doing all the things I'm "supposed" to do, which we call living life: I try to silence the scream inside my head which hasn't actually gone away. And because I'm so *well practised* in my "flip" into (so-called) "living life" I honestly don't think that other people know what's going on; they don't suspect the severity of my neediness (or selfishness). This adds fuel to my fear that if I were to "share" my burden, it might be too great to bear. You might not be able to bear it and you'd withdraw from me, or judge me, or label me. Or I might not be able to bear it either. Which is why I said: "And if I don't, I might have jumped off the merry-go-round of this world before I've had time to stop myself."

I don't know how to explain this very well. I don't know quite what to say. That's why I made a collage and I've brought it to show you. I think it speaks, you see. It tells. I think it describes things better than words can.

I folded the big sheet of paper as if I was making a greetings card. On the front I glued a picture of a teenage girl – she's fine-boned and beautiful – looking the picture of health and happiness. You can see, below, the headline saying that two weeks after this photograph was taken, the girl had killed herself. She couldn't bear the pressure inside her head ever since… ever since she told "everything" that had happened to her.

I know that feeling.

"Telling" does not necessarily bring relief.

When you turn the "card" over to the back, the biggest word you see is "FINISH". I cut it from an advert, but I hope you can tell that I meant that word in a different way. Beneath it there's that great big red "BYE BYE".

You must understand: it's not that I want to kill myself. It's just that I feel as if I've *got* to get away from this pressure. But the pressure is all on the inside. It's on the inside of me and the inside pages of this card. You haven't seen the reason for the pressure yet.

I put this picture of a baby on the back cover here, to show innocence and perhaps something angelic. Then I cut out different words from magazines and stuck them all around her: words describing heaven. They say:

PEACE OF MIND

REAL

PRECIOUS

TAKEN CARE OF

SOFT

WHITE

I was pleased about WHITE. That's what I always thought of to try to blank things out. I reckon white is the colour of blankness.

I need to be quiet.

In tiny writing, like a footnote at the very bottom of the page here, you can just read the cutting, "We regret to announce the sad demise…" I cut it off there, because this collage is for *my* story. It's not the story of someone else's sad demise.

I needed to take a big breath just then, in the middle of explaining this to you. You won't laugh at me, will you? I'm telling you about what's going on inside me, you see, and I don't normally tell other people this. So I need to be sure that you're not getting impatient or half-doing something else, before we open it out for the middle pages…

You're not rushing off, are you?

You can be quiet while I open it? Because it would be better for you not to look at all than for you to half-look when you're distracted.

I'm trusting you. I'll open it up now.

On the left-hand side of the inside page, the biggest thing is obviously that huge car, and beside it there's the word STOP.

I'm sure I don't need to say more, though you may not have noticed that here, on the *inside* of the car, it says HOPE AND LOVE. That was a bit cynical for me to put that there. It's what I thought Uncle George's car had in it. I went out with him so full of hope and love. I thought that was what he was giving.

If only I had realized… Why didn't I?

I don't understand myself. But anyway, let's go on.

All over this page are lots of small pictures of mouths smiling. I cut them out from their faces so all you can see is smiles. There are kind smiles and forced ones and smirking ones and laughing ones. Uncle George often smiled to me and I thought that meant he was friendly. I didn't know; I didn't know until I was making this collage that I must have got angry inside about all the smiles. But maybe I was angry at myself for smiling: smiling on the doorstep on Saturdays; smiling as I offered him tea and my home baking on Sundays; smiling to say thank you; smiling at school and at home to pretend to everyone that I was fine so no one would make a fuss or tell me off for being a silly girl.

Why did I keep smiling? Why didn't I ever "apply" for help? What happened?

I'm sorry; we'll never get through if I keep asking questions. I just want to point out these other words and phrases dotted all around this page; all around the smiles. They say:

SHOW HOW TO DO

CONTENTS: PERSONAL

KNICKERS WITH A TWIST

GET IN THERE. PURE BEAUTY

NARROW PASSAGE FULL

ESSENTIAL PLEASURES

LOOK NO FURTHER

And as you see, I cut up this word before I glued it on: INDIVIDUAL. It's all in fragments; little pieces.

That's me.

I'm all in pieces.

My life shattered, you know, just like one of those windscreens that don't just merely crack if they're hit but splinter into thousands of tiny pieces.

I need to take a moment to be quiet, please… just for a few seconds…

I know I shouldn't condemn myself but I feel so silly. Big breath in, Rose. Swallow. Blow my nose.

Thank you for not laughing at me.

Now, finally: the right-hand page. This is a bit stronger, really. There's the big black shape with only the small yellow type: THE SECRET IS CHILLING. And on top of that I've stuck the red lettering to ask, CULPRIT?

Those hands on their own – I put them straight underneath where it says, START. AN APPETISER.

. . . .

The words say:

BULLY

BEAT

CUT

FRANTIC

DON'T BITE

FIGHTING OFF

BIG BAD WOLF

INSIDE AND OUT

IT'S OK

THE WEEK AHEAD AND I STUCK BESIDE THAT, CHAOTIC

BETRAYAL

BITESIZE

RELAX

EXCELLENT BODY RIGIDITY

And all around are more smiles.

That one is very smug, don't you think?

I cut up WORTH on this page in exactly the same way as I had cut up INDIVIDUAL opposite. And in the corner, so it's the last thing you read before you turn over to the "heaven" page, I've stuck ENDS SOON next to HEAVEN. That's why there's that picture of the railway track there, beside, TO FINALLY FINISH IT OFF.

I'm putting my collage away now. You may think this is silly, but it's quite precious to me, this. I know I didn't take time over it but I felt satisfied as if I'd spent hours on it. I cut everything out with care, because it really was an expression of me. So as I put it away it's a bit like putting a baby to rest.

I'm only laughing to cover, you know. I'm embarrassed. I'm shy. I'm afraid in case you judge. But the truth is, I have to try really, really hard to stop myself from yielding to temptation. I know I'm not alone. Look at all the soldiers who came back from Vietnam and who couldn't bear life with such memories. More veterans committed suicide after the war than had died in it.[4] Look at Primo Levi who survived Auschwitz and wrote so emphatically and apparently wonderfully about the need to keep living, and after his "best" book, he killed himself. I bet that nobody would have known beforehand. All their deaths will have been a shock – why? Because we don't dare show what's inside. We hide; we cover ourselves with smiles so that what we can't bear is hidden. Then we wonder why we don't get help.

4   From *The Oxford Companion to American Military History*, ed. John Whiteclay Chambers II (New York: OUP, 1999).

31

This is the Story of My Beloved

I shall never forget the morning after I had dared to share the first of my drawings – my coded "confession" – with the tiny scrawled handwriting beneath some of them that looked more like a ten-year-old's script. I had woken up to a kaleidoscope of feelings within me and, although there was some relief along with the release, I was dismayed because my cupboard door had been prised open now, and I felt deep down that there was a finality about its opening so I could never close it completely again.

How right I was! Although I was frightened to death (yes, almost literally), I avoided my dismay by feeling angry instead.

I felt angry that something had been wheedled out of me that I'd wanted to keep a secret, even from myself.

I felt angry at myself for giving in.

I was furious that from now on I could be labelled: anything that I might have wrong with me could be put down to a hushed, "That'll be because she was abused."

I was angry because I'd cried: I'd sniffled and snivelled, and that didn't fit with how I wanted to see myself.

Most of all I was angry because I felt profoundly, totally, utterly humiliated.

Once my story had been told – even whispered, in confidence, to one person – something came to an end. I was afraid and sad and confused because, once denial is taken away, the consequences are enormous. Most obviously, from now on, I would no longer be allowed to think of myself as nice. I'd have to face the facts.

For example, words like "pink", and "feminine", and "dainty", and "nice" really would have to stay in the past tense, in relation to me – or so I felt. Those words belonged to Before. Before Uncle George.

Therefore, as I turned those pictures from one hand to another on that morning after drawing and writing tiny fragments of my story, I opened my hands, looking at the pages and I felt rather angry thoughts towards God. This, after all, was the God in whom I'd trusted forever. This was the God to whom I'd prayed from up the old oak tree. This was Jesus, my Friend, to whom I'd called out silently from the car while staring – desperately – at one raindrop. This was the God whom I'd begged to help me and show me how to face arriving back home when I really and truly didn't know how to begin to do so. I'd counted the lamp-posts knowing that Uncle George was driving me back, and I was nearing it, and what could I do... what could I do? From that panic, I had prayed to the God whom I knew to be a Good Shepherd, and I had trusted Him. Where was the good shepherding in all this, my story? I hadn't sketched even a half of it – oh, not a hundredth of it – but I'd penned enough for me to have an angry question in my mind. What, Lord, were You *do*ing?

Worst of all, this was Jesus, whom I had *loved*. I may have been very naïve but I had loved my Friend with all my heart. How could He have repaid me thus?

So I opened my hand and let my child-handwriting speak for itself. I didn't verbalize a question to God. The tears coursing down my cheeks spoke more loudly than words. I couldn't speak, myself.

I didn't know how God would respond to a cry like this. I didn't know what to expect. What I knew for sure was that I didn't want fake imaginings; I didn't want any religious fantasy. I wanted only reality. I wanted God and I wanted Him to be real. Would the two mix?

I sat down. The house was empty and therefore I allowed my tears to be slightly audible.

There are two chairs in my study and for some reason, I allowed myself to picture Jesus, as a man, sitting on the chair opposite mine. I knew I couldn't see Him with my physical eyes but I could picture Him. I looked in the direction of His chair and I think my facial expression might best be described as "glowering". (Granny would have been proud of me with my pursed lips.) I suspect I was almost daring Him to speak. Whatever He might begin to say, I was ready with an answer... Something like, "That doesn't help!" would have been sufficient.

The Jesus I was picturing did not speak.

My tears flowed a little more freely but now silently.

I must have been stunned, still, with the shock of hearing my own story. It had been an admission to myself, never mind anybody else. I say this because, in my stunned state, time passed more quickly than I really knew.

It must have been for about half an hour that I sat in my chair and Jesus, I imagined, sat in His. I felt as if He was resting His elbows on the arm-rests of the chair with His hands clasped, resting gently across His tummy. His pose was relaxed; just a little too relaxed for my comfort.

Eventually, I goaded provocatively, "Well?" I missed off the ending that I might have given, such as, "What do You have to say for Yourself then?" I hoped that my intonation spoke my hurt without my needing to sound too impertinent.

God's silence persisted for longer than I was comfortable with but, just before I got up to swish away in disgust at His uselessness, some words came into my mind that I can only say were not my own idea.

The voice was very gentle, and it was very honouring.

The words I heard were these: "This is the story of My beloved."

32

How Can This Be?

God can be incredibly tantalizing. He can allow silence to continue for an extraordinarily long time. For several years after that memorable day in my own study, I longed to hear more from Him. How did His story proceed? What came next? Come along, Lord; I was listening!

And then, Advent Sunday, 2004. Winchester Cathedral. Darkness; inky blackness punctuated only by a few candles, each casting a comma of light. The dance of each flame made a subtle suggestion to whoever-would-notice: Look! There is life even in a cold, tomb-like void. There is hope even in dreary winter bleakness. There is a dance; and the light does leap for joy, even (especially?) in the midst of darkness. But many would not have noticed that quiet, understated message.

A reading ended; the congregation coughed and shuffled until it settled back into a new stillness; the hush grew to anticipation. Alerted, we waited, craning our necks, straining our eyes and ears to catch the first nuance of what was about to happen.

For several seconds, there was nothing. The darkness and the silence became pregnant with anticipation.

Then, unseen, from around one corner – or possibly from one transept – a few notes rose, sung by the pure voices of the girls' choir. Their song became words; their words grew to a question. Because these were child-voices, they called for attention in a way that adults like myself have dulled by all our so-called "answers". I could hear the question, sung softly and honestly to God Himself.

"How can this be…?"

The brilliant clarity with which this choir enunciated their words left no space for non-comprehension. Oh, we knew what was being asked! And the very fact that the singers were young reinforced the simplicity of the question yet more, adding potency to the directness unique to children. Their pianissimo was transformed into a fortissimo shout.

As I heard, as I listened, I began to realize that the voice calling from the darkness was no longer merely the voice of a choir in the distance. This was my voice I was hearing, from the darkness right there, in which I was enveloped. *I* was the child. This was my question. I was asking it of God Himself.

"How can this be?"

As the prayer-song rose, like incense, those words ceased being only a quotation of words from the Bible. Oh yes, the choir was singing words of a girl who was "deeply troubled" by what was happening to her.[5] But the choir was doing far more than that, wreaking work within the very souls of the listeners, more deeply than we could have expected even from that pregnant hush before they began. They were giving expression to the question that every person in that cathedral would seek to ask of God, if they dared; if they were to find themselves before His throne.

However, the question was but the beginning of Tavener's piece.[6]

Suddenly from behind where I was seated, from another corner of the cathedral, I sensed a large, corporate intake of breath. The breathing alone informed me that the voices to follow were not those of the girls' choir. These were adult lungs being filled; large, male, big-barrelled chests. As they sang, this time the voice was not the high pitch of a child: bewildered, afraid, naïve. These

5   The whole story is contained in the Gospel of Luke, chapter 1.

6   *Annunciation*; John Tavener. Published by Chester Music.

were bass voices; strong adults; grown-ups; those who knew. They sang with utter confidence and resounding conviction. A tiny child had asked; now a knowing adult was replying. That male voice choir could have been the voice of God Himself.

"Hail!" The chord was full and irrefutable and arresting. "Hail!" There was a crescendo built in. Again, a third "Hail!" followed by a fourth and, loudest of all, a fifth, "Hail!"

Tavener, the composer of this piece, created such a strong sung-chord that the one-word greeting was almost an answer in itself. There scarcely needed to be more words – although they did follow. But that initial greeting – hail! – seemed to say, "Hello?" And the second time, "Yes, this is Me – God – speaking to you; yes, you!" Then the third time, "Hello!" And again, "Are you listening?" I felt as if God, frustrated by years of my non-hearing, took me by the lapels to drum His truth into me, time after time: "Listen! I am addressing *you*!"

After grabbing my attention, those bass voices – the God-voice – became more gentle, meandering around both harmony and melody as they declared softly, "You are highly favoured."

So involved had I become that the words were being spoken to me. Not only was God asking for my attention: now He was telling me, "You are highly favoured."

Could I believe Him? Could I – would I – receive such reassurance?

Tears rolled silently down my cheeks as I heard, and acknowledged, but could not yet absorb. Why, to do so would alter my whole view of life!

As if the choir – or Tavener – understood that I could not yet believe it properly, the high voices sang again their quiet, bewildered, disorientated reply, repeating the original dismay:

"How can this be…?"

Once again I could not identify the exact location of the singers. Once again I knew that this question wound its way both from a hidden transept of the cathedral and also from some distant corridor of my mind.

Then again the bass voices – the God-voice – came in, declaring this time, "The Lord is with thee."

And again came the incredulous, "How can this be…?"

Finally, a third time, the voice of God rang out with yet more conviction, more confidence than before. "Blessed art thou among women."

Yet, despite all the confidence, all the strength, despite the irrefutable conviction of the God-voice, still the bewilderment had not been dispelled. Yet again the music returned to the child-voices, more hushed now, but continuing as if eternally on this earth. It was with the question, not the answer, that *The Annunciation* ended.

Thus the question remained, echoing around both Winchester Cathedral and the recesses of my own mind. The light of the last candles exited with the choir. We, the body of the church, were left in darkness and in silence. The stillness was pronounced and prolonged. Unlike previously, there were no shuffling coughs. We knew we'd been touched by an eternal truth that we could not comprehend. Nobody wanted to be first to break its hold on us.

That question rings on. We need no artificial light to reveal it to us: perhaps we hear it better from darkness. It is there, in the world. It is here, within me. With all that has happened, despite all of God's promises, I do not understand. I have had glimpses of God, yes, for which I am truly thankful and without which I would not still be here. But I am still journeying, still asking the question that I'm certain that God accepts – even honours – even though many humans find it almost impossible. And my question is this: How can it be that God sees my story as the story of His beloved? How can it be that He watched, and allowed, and did not restrain Uncle George? How can it be that He heard my prayers, my heartfelt, child prayers, and He still hung back from doing something?

How can that be?

I have heard the beginning of God's "answer". I have heard that He addresses me. "Hail!" And although I have yet to absorb the full significance of Him speaking to me, I bow my head, awed because He speaks. That is a beginning. With one word He quiets my restless soul.

Then, "The Lord is with thee" – God's oft-repeated promise, made to every human universally. The Bible is peppered with the words, "The Lord is with thee." And though I know He offers this as His promise, can I really trust it to be more than a spiritual fantasy?

Do I believe Him?

When I feel alone and I crave help and human contact, how much can I turn my mind and heart to apply what I heard in Winchester Cathedral?

Can I hear these words as God's *promise*?

Although Mary had her special place in history that no other woman may claim, what about those words, "Thou art highly favoured"? Does God address every person in almost the same way? When He repeatedly declares that He loves us; when in an entire book of the Bible I read about "His beloved", can I believe Him? Can I be sure He's addressing me?

If He is our heavenly Father, can I go as far as to believe that *He* might address me as His "Darling Daughter"?

Epilogue

Uncle George went to his grave without anyone else knowing what had happened. He was not tried or convicted.

In mid-life, Rose was no longer able to suppress the truth of what had happened during her childhood. Aching for some support, she told her mother. Her mother did not know how to make sense of what she was hearing. She was shocked and confused. How could Uncle George have done such dreadful things, when *she* had known him to have been a kind man? He was the church warden who had paid Rose's school fees. The story was impossible to reconcile.

In her distress, she called Rose a "slut" for saying dirty things, crying out, "I can't bear this!" Rose's brothers agreed that she should not be expected to do so. They were angry that their mother had been upset and, together, the whole family insisted that Rose be silent on this matter. It was made clear that she was not welcome in the family unless she undertook never to speak of this again… not the pain, nor the nightmares that she continued to experience.

Miss Flowers (the Latin teacher), however, came closer to Rose. Her first words were, "So *that's* what it was!" She had attributed Rose's desire to stand close to her desk as a teenage girl's crush. Rose felt soothed and comforted by the sincerity of Miss Flowers' apology, even though it came so many decades late. She showed care and respect for Rose – which Rose found very healing. And then Miss Flowers died.

Rose's childhood hunch proved to have been correct. She had ruminated, many times, "Mummy mustn't know…"

And Now *You* Know...

And now *you* know.

You may be thinking, "Help! What do I do now?"

The worst thing you could do is to sigh, "Poor Rose!", shelve the book (and the subject), and pick up life as before.

But you may be prickling with discomfort.

You may know an adult "Rose". Or you yourself may be a "Rose".

You may know a child who you think could be a "Rose".

You may wonder if a friend or colleague could be an "Uncle George".

You may be an "Uncle George" (or "Auntie…") and you may want help.

You may be worried about how effective your safeguarding policy is – specifically if you are part of an organization involving contact with children.

You may simply feel that your knowledge is so limited that you're paralysed, not knowing what to do, but you've now been woken up to the fact that abuse is happening today, now, right under our noses.

Many organizations offer help and support in various forms for people touched by the issues raised in this book – too many to list here. But how does one choose where to turn?

The following pages give details about an organization that I can certainly recommend, namely **CCPAS** (Churches' Child Protection Advisory Service; 0845 120 4550; www.ccpas.co.uk).

The **NSPCC** (National Society for the Prevention of Cruelty to Children; 0808 800 5000; www.nspcc.org.uk) has an excellent website and is particularly helpful if you are concerned about a child.

NAPAC (National Association for People Abused in Childhood; 0800 085 3330; www.napac.org.uk) exists to support survivors of child abuse when they want to talk and receive support. They know that most children who are abused don't talk about it until they become adults.

Preventing and responding to abuse

CCPAS (Churches' Child Protection Advisory Service) exists to safeguard children and vulnerable adults throughout the UK. It also works to help those throughout the UK who are being, or have been, harmed by child abuse. Founded in 1977, CCPAS is the only independent Christian safeguarding charity, and it provides:

- a 24-hour confidential helpline
- professional training and advice
- disclosure checks
- safeguarding policies and updates
- support and resources.

CCPAS has pioneered many policies that have now been adopted by major denominations, other faith and non-faith organizations. It also advises the UK government, safeguarding boards, children's social care, adult social services, the police, the probation service, the health service, voluntary bodies, and other agencies across the UK.

To do this, CCPAS depends on its team of highly experienced and skilled professionals, all of whom have high levels of expertise that extend across a wide range of professions and backgrounds. These include social workers and counsellors who have decades of collective experience in the field. They are knowledgeable, practical, and approachable.

. . . .

Help after abuse

When abuse happens it can have a ripple effect on family, friends, places of worship, and the wider community. In these circumstances, CCPAS can offer on-going support, including one-to-one meetings with those concerned.

CCPAS runs a helpline twenty-four hours a day, seven days a week. Since it began over thirty years ago it has been a source of comfort and support for literally thousands of people hurting from abuse, or the consequences of abuse.

Everybody is welcome to use the helpline. It serves individuals such as parents, children and young people, and adults. It is also available to church leaders, organizations, social workers, local safeguarding children boards, and other professional bodies.

Many survivors of abuse contact CCPAS for specialist support and advice. These people have found to be very useful the CCPAS series of *Help!* leaflets, and other relevant material, which may be downloaded from the website or ordered by post from CCPAS, PO Box 133, Swanley, Kent BR8 7UQ.

CCPAS responds with compassion because its staff have much experience in dealing with this issue. So they listen and, when appropriate, refer to local counselling agencies. Their help is *offered* not *forced*. Those who have availed themselves of CCPAS speak very highly of their experienced help.

CCPAS can be followed on Facebook, Twitter and through their website and safeguarding blog.

Help for Those Outside the UK

Australia

Lifeline is a national charity offering 24-hour crisis support (www.lifeline.org.au; 13 11 14). This telephone number may be used from all over Australia by anyone who feels in danger, or who believes a child may be in danger.

. . . .

Kids Helpline (www.kidshelp.com.au; 1800 55 1800) offers free and confidential counselling to children in need of help.

South Africa

There are various non-government organizations – for example www.rapcan.org.za (**Resources Aimed at the Prevention of Child Abuse and Neglect**) – that are active in South Africa.

Rape Crisis (www.rapecrisis.org.za) has branches country-wide and aims to support and empower rape victims as well as raise awareness.

The organization **WMACA** (Women and Men Against Child Abuse; http://wmaca.org.za) aims specifically to help fight for the rights of victims of child abuse.

Childline South Africa (http://childlinesa.org.za; 08000 55 555) offers a free 24-hour helpline for children.

New Zealand

Telephone number 0508 326 459 is a Freephone number that ANY PERSON may phone who suspects child abuse or neglect, or who is worried about a child or young person. There are also the following organizations in New Zealand:

Kidshealth (www.kidshealth.org.nz/child-abuse-information-and-support) provides an extensive listing of organizations, resources, helplines, and counselling services.

Child Matters (www.childmatters.org.nz; (07) 838 3370) is a charity that provides guidance, advice, education, and support to those in a position to act to protect children. Their training and education programmes provide adults with essential skills, and just as importantly the confidence, to intervene when a child needs help. By the end of 2013, Child Matters had trained over 21,000 adults in New Zealand in how to recognize and respond to child abuse.

Jigsaw (www.jigsaw.org.nz) is a not-for-profit organization focused on the wellbeing of all New Zealand children and their families. The diverse group of independent, community-based social service agencies that make up the Jigsaw network advocate against all forms of child abuse, neglect, and family violence, and provide support to families so they can raise their children in safe and nurturing ways.

United States of America

National Children's Alliance (www.nationalchildrensalliance. org) is a professional membership organization that puts the needs of child victims first. It is dedicated to helping local communities to respond to allegations of child abuse in ways that are effective and efficient. It provides training, support, technical assistance, and leadership on a national level to local children's and child advocacy centres and communities, responding to reports of child abuse and neglect. A children's advocacy centre is a child-focused, facility-based programme in which representatives from many disciplines, including law enforcement, child protection, prosecution, mental health, medical and victim advocacy, and child advocacy, work together to conduct interviews and make team decisions about investigation, treatment, management, and prosecution of child abuse cases.

Hong Kong

CRIN (Child Rights Information Network) has a branch in Hong Kong: www.aca.org.hk. Action against Child Abuse works for the removal of all forms of child abuse and child neglect in Hong Kong; to establish, maintain, and support a professional service which can deal with abused or neglected children, or parents who have problems with their children; to promote awareness of the prevention of child abuse.

The website http://www.crin.org/reg/country.asp?ctryID=14 &subregID=18 includes resources organized alphabetically by country.

About Jane Grayshon

Jane Grayshon, author of nine books, trained as a nurse and midwife, but illness prevented her from pursuing clinical work, despite her love of it. She first wrote a textbook for nurses, *Obstetric & Gynaecological Nursing*, but then she turned to writing more personally. Her *Confessions of a Vicar's Wife* is a hilarious anthology of her weekly broadcasts on BBC Radio Merseyside, in which she describes her life as a clergy wife: how had she put her foot in things *this* week?! This was hotly pursued by another volume, *Vicar's Wife on the Move*, in which Jane discloses the chronology of events that are normally kept highly secret when vicars move (and, as Jane points out, "It happens that the wife moves, too, don't forget!").

Nevertheless, Jane's most significant writing is found in her more serious works: *A Pathway Through Pain* which, having first been published in 1987, has now been described as a Christian classic. Compellingly written, she describes her own experience of unrelenting pain, her repeated prayer begging God to cure her, and her discovery that healing is very different from cure. This book has led to hundreds of people writing to Jane, expressing their astonishment, relief and gratitude, because "at last someone [Jane] has put into words what I have experienced yet nobody has seemed to understand." It is not surprising therefore that *A Pathway Through Pain* has been reprinted several times; three editions in the UK, and it has been translated into several languages.

A Pathway Through Pain was followed by other books, including *Treasures of Darkness*, in which Jane explores the gifts that are formed by, and discovered in, times of darkness. Among her earlier books is *Faith in Flames*, a book of her most poignant poems that quietly contain the implicit message that, sadly, Jane knows what it means to be sexually abused. Her interest in survivors of sexual abuse was awoken in 1992 when, as a broadcaster on BBC Radio 4, she presented a general feature in which she chaired a group discussion on the subject. During her preparation she met "Rose" (a pseudonym), whose story awoke in Jane a deep empathy. Rose had read Jane's *A Pathway Through Pain*. Their mutual recognition of the depths that they shared led to a bond of friendship that has grown deeper over the years.

* * *

Of all her books, Jane describes *Goodbye Pink Room* as the most difficult to write but she drew creatively from her midwifery experience. "To write Rose's story is the most precarious delivery I have ever undertaken," Jane explains. This is because, in order to bring the book to birth, Jane needed to win the trust of "Rose", whose vulnerable fragility became increasingly evident with every word she uttered.

"Writing about Rose has proved to be a huge privilege in my life," says Jane. "She is the person above all others who has taught me that there is no shame in being fragile, and that there's something very precious within our vulnerability."